101

Things to do
with a

Retired Man

to get him out from under your feet

AN HACHETTE UK COMPANY

www.hachette.co.uk

First published in Great Britain in 2012 by Spruce
a division of Octopus Publishing Group Ltd, Carmelite House,
50 Victoria Embankment, London EC4Y 0DZ

www.octopusbooks.co.uk | www.octopusbooksusa.com

This edition published in 2018.

Text and Design © Octopus Publishing Group Ltd 2012, 2018

Illustrations © Sophie Joyce 2012, 2018

Additional illustrations by Jasper Wake age 3.5

Distributed in the US by Hachette Book Group USA
1290 Avenue of the Americas, 4th and 5th Floors
New York NY 10104 USA

Distributed in Canada by Canadian Manda Group
664 Annette Street, Toronto, Ontario, Canada, M6S 2C8

ISBN 978-1-846-01556-4

A CIP catalogue record for this book is available from the
British Library

Printed and bound in China

10 9 8 7 6 5 4 3 2 1

NOTES

This book contains the opinions and ideas of the author.
The author and the publisher disclaim all responsibility for
any liability, any loss, or any risk, personal or otherwise,
incurred as a consequence, directly or indirectly, of the use
and application of any of the contents of this book.

Gabrielle Mander
Illustrated by
Sophie Joyce

101
Things to do
with a
Retired Man
to get him out from under your feet

Today's the day! It's Monday, 7.00 am and you are wide-awake, although for the first time in four decades the alarm didn't kick-start your heart. What is that sound? Could it be birdsong, for once not drowned out by the power shower? If you listen carefully, you can also hear the Hawaiian shirts and Bermuda shorts jostling to get to the front, revving up to party. Sixty is the new forty, eighty the new sixty (but 100 is still 100, because, wow—that's old).

There are worlds to conquer and this is the time to have the time of your lives! Sunny days and heady nights await you, not just for two weeks each year, but forever! You've been looking forward to this happy-ever-after time together, so why are you both peeping over the quilt, white-knuckled with anxiety? Now he has retired, what will he do all day? What will you talk about? There are only so many times he can mow the lawn, walk the dog, and paint the fence. This isn't a vacation; this is the rest of his life, and yours—scary, huh?

With decades of free time ahead of him, remind him of the man he was (and still is) before his head was full of money and meetings, customers and cutbacks, bottom lines, or boardroom battles. The time has come to decide what he wants to be. *101 Things to do with a Retired Man* is designed to help you inspire and tease him into having the time of his life, and to fill his days with sometimes silly, sometimes useful, but always interesting things to do. These do not include lying on the sofa, watching daytime television, measuring the height of the blades of grass, redecorating the bathroom, or restacking the dishwasher in the most efficient fashion as apparently only a man can. (You could always get your own back by sneakily turning the knives upside down, but frankly, that's for another book.) Welcome instead to the real world of places waiting to be discovered, lights crying out to be taken out from under bushels, (whatever bushels may be) and a sense of the ridiculous lurking in the corner, longing to tickle you into enjoying the rest of your lives.

Be a little patient though. This transition can be daunting and man will need time to adjust, so start him off gently. Press that fine pen he received as a retirement present into service as he writes a list of all the things he would like to do. Review it together. If he wants to paint, don't give him a box of watercolours and a beret; get him some spray cans and a hoodie and encourage him to customize your garage wall! Is he adventurous? Buy him some stout walking boots and a flashlight (alright, make him a cape, if you must) and send him out as Urbex Man: urban explorer.

On wet days he could make fashion items from great moments in history: The Gettysburg address for example (how hard can it be to knit your own Abe Lincoln?) If golf is his thing, encourage him to play all the major golf courses in the land. It could take months. Has he only used his voice to say "Yes, Sir, No, Sir" for the past forty years? Now is the time for him to take back the power, sing out, and even join a choir. Is he a master map-reader? Introduce him to geocaching, (You will have to read on).

"What about our responsibilities?" I hear you cry! Perhaps you have grandchildren. Include them in your plans. They may not appreciate your new tattoos—kids can be such killjoys—but they will love visiting the seven wonders of the world, riding the rollercoasters, or dipping their toes in the ocean! So hide his carpet slippers! Let him learn mime or Mandarin, open a hedgehog hospital, or take up tiny topiary. The world is definitely his and of course, your oyster!

Conservation piece

In his prime, Man the Hunter brings home the metaphorical bacon—unless he's bringing home literal bacon, in which case you have yourself a keeper. When your hunter retires, he may be ready to take a gentler look at the world around him. Man the Conservationist might well find he has the time and inclination to offer a helping hand to some other of God's creatures who are at a crossroads—or otherwise facing challenges in their lives.

Antelopes and wildebeest may roam wild in your neighborhood. However, remain calm. He doesn't have to bring his charges home (unless they're bacon) and no one has to cook them (unless, again, bacon), so you can afford to be supportive. Encourage him to look into nature clubs and societies for local conservation projects.

Activites might include checking dolphin populations off the coast, or guarding rare birds' nests from predators. Many locales boast toads and frogs that need to cross a busy road and could do with a subway, or, at the very least, a sign asking motorists to slow down. Get him to paint a sign promising motorists the transformation of frogs into princes!

Turtles laying their eggs on the
beach in Northern Florida need
stalwart men to protect them
from becoming sunny-side up
and then to help the babies to
the sea. Many tiny turtles fall
into the moats of sandcastles
and need rescuing! Even
the stoniest heart melts
at the chance to rescue
tidbit-sized turtles from
terrible fates. And he'll
need someone to go
to Florida
with him...

And another thing...

Is your man becoming grumpier by the day? Now that he is separated from his fellow rat racers on the 7:25, he has only you to be his grumblee. It is the preliminary shake of the newspaper, followed by the deep sigh, "Have you seen this...?" that the long-suffering partner of a retiree most dreads. It promises a long rant on the state of the economy, education, or the idiocy of the football coach who has failed yet again!

To counter his Grumpy Old Man morning ritual, plan the mother of all ranting parties.

To counter his Grumpy Old Man morning ritual, plan the mother of all ranting parties. Construct a small rostrum, or use a grassy knoll, to raise the ranter above the revelers. Invite your friends and neighbors and supply great music, delicious food, and flowing wine to gird them for the glorious ire to come.

Provide a fetching hat and cloak, and explain that whoever dons them must ascend the speaker's post and express his or her discontent, in no uncertain terms, on any aspect of modern life. Fellow guests may interject, throw tomatoes, or otherwise heckle. You will find both your home and the produce aisle of your local supermarket to be calmer and gentler places in the days that follow. Though tomatoes may be in short supply.

Chains, my baby's got me locked up...

It is unlikely, but possible, that now he has retired, you sometimes find your soul mate just the tiniest bit irritating (this may even be mutual, not that either of you would ever admit it). Yes, you love him to pieces, but you are, after all, together 24 hours a day. Consider escapology. This is not to suggest that he should proceed straight to full immersion in a tank of water, his shivering body bound in chains of cold, hard steel, fastened with a dozen padlocks, whilst you look on, (laughing). the key dangling tantalizingly from your outstretched hand. Although he might be game, if it got you into elbow-length gloves and a plumed headdress.

Escapology for beginners involves only those things he has cherished since boyhood: a working knowledge of knots, a length of rope, and some talent for duplicity and distraction. Dig out that spare strait jacket too. If you don't have a strait jacket, make one together as a fun craft (this lesson to be covered in *An Additional 101 Things to Do with a Retired Man*). The internet has many magic sites with video instructions in simple technique. Many famous escapologists, like the great Harry Houdini, learned from a book but classes teaching magic and circus skills are available in most major cities.

It's been said that escapology is a metaphor for casting off the frustrations of modern life. Just the ticket for a bored retiree, eh?

Meet the ancestors

In the glow of the embers of what used to to be his briefcase and brogues, you catch your guy gazing into the distance, contemplating his own mortality. Nip this smartly in the bud; he should be looking to his promising future, inspired by the legacy of his family's past.

Suggest that he take up the study of genealogy to discover his deepest roots and the extraordinary history that lies behind every ordinary family. With the names and details of his earliest known ancestors in hand, there are many great public records to start with, many of which are online: birth registries, marriage certificates, death announcements, census reports, and church memberships. There are so many genealogy sites to choose from that it is difficult to recommend one over another, but most are genuinely useful.

Family stories and anecdotes too, often hold profound truths at their heart, even if details have become blurred over time. (See, he told you he was of royal blood; his noble ancestor was stolen as a baby by goblins and given to poor but honest peasants!) His online quest may well lure him to a physical location where he can touch original documents and photographs. This can be a powerful, moving experience, so have that monogrammed handkerchief, found in the tiny fist of the stolen infant, ready.

The Prestige

A man who produces rabbits out of hats, coins from behind ears, and doves from beneath velvet cloths will always be in demand at parties. Now he has more time, and possibly less contact with old workmates and colleagues, your social life will take on new significance and he will want to make a bit of a splash. If the number of his friends is diminishing, he will be charmed by the opportunity to swap the social circle for the magic one.

Sartorially, this one is a winner. Think how handsome he will look in top hat and tails and this is the best excuse yet for a silk-lined cape. Prestidigitation, or the quickness of the hand deceiving the eye, has hidden benefits for the older man. As with all success it takes a great amount of practice to become proficient at conjuring, and apart from the free time that you will enjoy your own pursuits, his practice will do wonders for stiffening joints. Card tricks require an excellent memory, warding off "senior moments," and will come in useful when you hit the casinos later in his retirement. Start with a simple box of conjuring tricks, and a magic wand, progressing in complexity until he's pulling a rabbit out of a top hat.

The Phoenix and the Carpet Slippers

Your guy has traced his family history and everyone agrees that Great, Great, Uncle Henry absolutely did not deserve that prison stretch! On the other hand, what about Emily, Countess of Othershire, lady-in-waiting to the Virgin Queen? This is what we genealogists call ancestor offset: for every black sheep there is a noble scion lurking in the upper branches of the family tree. We don't have to be related to a Knight of the Round Table to celebrate the 57 varieties of our personal histories in a coat of arms and family crest. A portcullis representing that prison door which banged behind Uncle Henry could be flanked by cigarettes rampant to show Emily's "close friendship" with Sir Walter Raleigh, incorporating "bezants", "plates", "hurts", and perhaps even a "bagwin" or two! If your family can't afford bezants or bagwins, substitute with lemon juice, which removes most any stain, even on reputations.

Encourage him to use all his creativity and wit to express his family tree in the symbolism of heraldry. He can study heraldic symbols and design his own crest at your local library, or use the trusty (if not always trustworthy) internet! The final design can be cast in a signet ring or family seal, which could become an heirloom to baffle future generations. Isn't baffling tradition what legacy is all about?

Play up and play the game

It is possible, but unlikely that your chap has reached retirement age without taking a passing interest in a sport. Perhaps he has played—and still plays, albeit more slowly—baseball, rugby, or football? Or maybe his tastes run to some lesser known sport, like trout-hurling? (We don't recommend it.) It is less likely that he has been able to follow these games in the professional arena (or river, in the trout's case).

Now that he has time, he could do worse than to challenge his prejudices and exult in sporting activities from the stands. It's time to consider a career as a soccer hooligan. Wait! Maybe not that drastic a commitment. How about just a fan? Even the most bookish among us is secretly drawn to the big matches, the cup finals, and the World Series. It is exhilarating to watch true professionals at the top of their game, feel the excitement in the air, and drink in the atmosphere (and beer) at a live match.

Your man's challenge is to be a spectator at as many professional games, matches, and events, in as wide a variety of sports as he can enjoy. Geography may be a challenge, but with luck he will have some kind of subsidized travel pass to ease the burden on his pocket (see page 33). He will enjoy researching the possibilities and drawing up a short list of events to get him started.

Man wonder-maker

Has breakfast become boring; home life humdrum? Surprise your man: challenge him over the Cheerios to name the seven man-made wonders of the world. Be warned, it's like trying to remember the names of the seven dwarves. Most of us falter at Dopey or Grumpy (which are fitting), and in this age of wonders, his list might be contentious, including the internet, the large Hadron Collider, satellites, spacecraft, even the mobile phone. But your objective is to get him to think big and then walk the walk.

For the record, traditionally, the seven wonders of the ancient world would be the Great Pyramid of Giza, the Hanging Gardens of Babylon, the Statue of Zeus at Olympia, the Temple of Artemis at Ephesus, the Mausoleum of Mausolos at Halicarnassus, the Colossus of Rhodes, and the Lighthouse of Alexandria. B-list wonders might include Stonehenge, the Coliseum, the Catacombs of Kom el Shoqafa, the Great Wall of China, the Porcelain Tower of Nanjing, Hagia Sophia, and the Leaning Tower of Pisa.

He might propose the Golden Gate Bridge, the CN Tower, the Panama Canal, the Channel Tunnel, or the Itaipu Dam. When you have marked his work, and soothed his ruffled feathers, your mission, should you choose to accept it, is to visit seven of them! At the very least, you will have brightened up breakfast.

Eak-spay ou-yay ig-Pay atin-Lay?

Is your man fluent in many tongues, not including profanity and grunting? He might have learned a foreign language or two at school, or picked up business French, German, or Japanese in the course of his working life. Would he feel comfortable in a foreign land when it comes to more than "How much is that?" and "My friend is paying?" Travelling all over the world has never been easier or more affordable and he could use his newfound leisure time to explore the culture, cuisine, and lifestyle of foreign lands.

Why not offer an incentive? Promise him that if he gains a working knowledge of the language of a country of his choice within six months, you will reward him with a short break for you both in that land. (It's a chore for you of course, taking an exotic holiday).

First, he must choose his destination, which could take some time and beware, his decision might not be Paris or Venice. The deal is if he talks the talk, he gets to walk the walk anywhere—from China to Iceland, Turkestan to Swaziland, and a million places in between. He can tackle his lessons with any language resource available, from online tutorials or discs, to old-fashioned textbooks and evening classes, but reciting "The cabbage of my aunt is very pregnant" will not win the golden ticket.

Cabin fever

Call it what you will—cabin, shed, or outhouse—many a man, retired or not, feels the need to establish an outpost between the great outdoors and the comforts of home. This is his domain, where he can "work" on projects, read the newspaper, have a few beers, spill oil, and spread sawdust where no one will give him grief. After a lifetime of weekend chores, his refuge could probably do with a makeover. Men being men, this notion is now a competitive sport.

Encourage your guy to channel his inner interior designer, clear out the cobwebs and old cans, and create his very own space where he can be at one with himself. He (or a qualified electrician) can install a power supply (perhaps solar?) and a wireless router so he can access the internet in peace. If he doesn't have a shed, look at the fantastic garden buildings on offer, from shepherd's huts on wheels to eco-design home offices, and buy him one as a retirement present.

Once he has his space, he should let his imagination run free. Maybe he harbors secret dreams of a sheik's tent with flowing silks and oriental carpets, or a pioneer's cabin with rough-hewn furniture and a pot-bellied stove? Perhaps he will recreate his bedroom from the 1960s? The lawn mower will have to find another home.

URBEX-MAN

For the adventurous retired man the urban jungle holds few surprises. He has walked its mean streets and fed its feral ducks on the municipal duck ponds. He knows its broad thoroughfares and winding lanes like the back of his hand. Or does he?

Hardcore urban exploration (Urbex or UE) seeks out the normally unseen or off-limits. He will need sensible clothing and light waterproof gear, a decent pair of walking boots, a good quality flashlight, a detailed street map (put one on his smartphone so he can call you for help deciphering it), and most of all: a real sense of adventure.

This style of urbex is not for the faint-hearted. Your retiree will need to be a bit of a rebel and physically fit to take part.

Targets might include abandoned buildings, sewers, and catacombs, or utility and transit tunnels. This style of urbex is not for the faint-hearted. Your retiree will need to be a bit of a rebel and physically fit, and he may risk bodily danger and potential prosecution for trespass, both of which will remind you of the thrilling bad boy you fell in love with.

Start with Urbex–lite. Get permission from civil authorities or the owner of a "ghost building" and sign an insurance waiver to thus enter the premises perfectly legally. The true thrill should be in discovery and some good photographs, not in any kind of vandalism or criminality! Unless you are wedded to a retired gentleman thief...

The case of the forgotten town

Your guy has spent a lifetime departing home at dawn and returning at dusk. Now it is important he reconnect with his hometown, or, if you are relocating, that you both get the lay of the land. Obviously Watson, the best way to do this is to don a deerstalker hat, clench a meerschaum pipe between his teeth, and take a murder mystery walk.

To devise his own walk, he will need to do a town survey, following a logical route (lovely!) around town, noting landmarks, dates on storefronts or municipal hardware, blue plaques of notable events or birthplaces, war memorials, tombstones, sundials, and dedications on park benches. Using these, and a planned route, he should devise names and cryptic clues or anagrams for 10 murder suspects with rough sketches and a separate list of 5 possible weapons, Clue/Cluedo-style. The clues will enable the "detective" to eliminate the innocent and uncover the murderer. Numerical clues (from dates etc.) will match the weapons and be eliminated separately. By the time the detective has solved the crime, he will have exercised mind and body, clocking up a good 2-to-3 mile walk.

Not only will he learn the town history, he will be able to send friends off in pursuit of the same quest. Most importantly, he will have another hat to add to his collection.

My Life in Pictures

If he has traced his genealogy as directed on page 10, Retired Man will not need you to tell him how vital even the tiniest scrap of information can be when trying to picture the daily lives of his ancestors. Nevertheless, do remind him of that (it doesn't count as nagging) when you suggest he record for posterity his own wonderful, frustrating, successful life. It will give him a chance to edit those embarrassing pictures of himself naked on a bearskin rug aged two, and later, in loon pants and a headband, making the peace sign, man.

He should probably leave out the sheep rustling, the cheerleader, and the "not inhaling" from his biography but that's all.

He can create a PowerPoint presentation or use an online bookmaker (no bets involved) to make a lavish personal and family history for his children and his children's children.

If he can imagine how extraordinary it would be to hear his own great-great grandfather's voice, he might make an audio version of his recollections. He should leave out the sheep rustling, the cheerleader, and not inhaling from his biography, but that's all. Tickets and line-ups from concerts and gigs, diplomas and school reports, his travels and his triumphs, and his disappointments, should feature and you may not edit out your embarrassing hairstyles either.

Move over Fabergé

It is imperative, if your man is to enjoy his retirement, that he does not have time to brood, and it is your role to watch carefully for the signs. When the rain is splashing in the gutters you must have at your fingertips some surprising, all-absorbing alternative to the daily crossword and Sudoku; an unexpected stimulant to capture his imagination.

Your larder or refrigerator may provide the very means you seek to distract and delight him, in the form of common hen's eggs. Later, when he becomes proficient in the art revealed here, he can vary his creations with goose, duck or quail, but for beginners, stick with an egg plentiful enough to destroy. He will also need vegetable or food dyes, adhesive, tweezers, and cocktail sticks or toothpicks to attach these decorations to the surface of his eggs. You may also provide sequins and glitter, since no man possesses these things or would even admit to knowing what sequins are.

The challenge is in working with the fragile shells without breaking them. The solution is to blow them. A pinhole is made in each end and the contents blown gently into a suitable receptacle. While he decorates the empty shells with gemstones to rival the legendary Fabergé eggs of Imperial Russia, you could whip up a priceless lunch of smoked salmon and scrambled eggs.

Pass it on

Recycling is the buzzword of our age. Once your man has separated the plastics from the paper, composted the leftovers, and taken the bottles to the bottle bank (nobody's counting), he could look to recycling a lifetime's knowledge, wisdom, and experience of a working life. Did he run his own business and could he advise a start-up company? Does he possess accountancy skills?

Young people sometimes find it difficult to accept the advice of their own parents or grandparents, but a smart chap like yours could really give them a boost. Local chambers of commerce and branch banks may recommend him to new businesses that could do with his help. If you've allowed him to keep a couple of business suits in his cupboard, he will scrub up nicely

Schools and literacy classes welcome those with time and talent to share.

when he turns up to volunteer to mentor the next generation. Also, in these cash-strapped times, schools and literacy classes welcome those with time and talent to help children or adults read, or improve their numeracy skills. After all as the saying should go: "Those who can, do. Those who could, teach."

Wonderful, naturally

Okay so the seven wonders of the ancient world may be a little difficult to visit in the 21st century, but every nation boasts its own glorious landmarks. Planning your vacations around them can be a truly fascinating, satisfying experience. Go and see the Northern Lights or your local Wonder of the World (every country's got one). Snowdonia in Wales is well worth a visit, not to mention The Giant's Causeway in Northern Ireland. Europe boasts wonders, like Germany's Black Forest or France's Ardeche Gorge.

In the USA, you can hardly go a couple of thousand miles without tripping over the Mojave Desert, the Grand Canyon, or Niagara Falls. In Australia you can explore the Great Barrier Reef or climb Ayers Rock. (Make a day of it with a picnic! Or take a walkabout in the bush!) Half the fun is in finding the exotic and awe-inspiring for yourselves.

Your retired man will want to execute this trip properly with meticulous planning and research. An adventure awaits you of spinning globes and maps with little colored pins, road trips, bicycles to be rented, and flight schedules to be studied. He can blog his way around the country and post the pictures on Facebook! He'll love it, and so will you; he chooses the wonders and you pick the wonderful B&Bs.

Your country needs you

"**A**sk not what your country can do for you—ask what you can do for your country." Write these inspiring words from President John F. Kennedy on a stack of post-it notes and stick them wherever your man cannot miss them. Be prepared to dodge the missiles that he may feel obliged to throw at you, then sit him down and draw up a "nice" list of ways in which he might serve the civic need.

Many a man is a fool for a badge and a pair of Ray-Bans; it's the Sheriff of Dodge City syndrome. He might be attracted to life on the streets volunteering as a "special" with his local police force. The fire department may well have need of someone to man the phones or undertake some other duty. If he is the cerebral type or just enjoys shushing others, he could volunteer at his local library. Or he could help out with census or local election administration.

Many a man is a fool for a badge and a pair of Ray-Bans...

The elderly or disabled often need reliable drivers to bus them to their errands and appointments. Your local civic hall lists organizations seeking volunteers, and the ubiquitous internet will also carry such information. If he is considering becoming a school crossing supervisor you'll know—you'll see the signs!

If a picture paints a thousand words

Yes, yes, you're quite right, there was a version of this classic number spoken by Telly Savalas in the 1970s, but that, mercifully, is another story. This story is about how your man can fill his newly-minted free time with creative pursuits for pleasure and profit. Does he have a talent with charcoal, brush, or pen? Can he catch the fleeting likeness of a bird on the wing, or a pooch by the fireside? Does he have the insight for self-portraiture or the diplomacy to paint pictures of others? Yes? Then buy him a smock and a beret and set him to work. No? Then it is time he enrolled in some life classes and learned.

As well as classes in technique, drawing, and painting, he should take a course in art appreciation and another in the history of art. You could join him in this and enhance his studies with trips to the great cities of Renaissance Europe, ostensibly to view the Great Masters, although you may feign surprise to learn that Florence and Paris also offer outstanding food and wine. Perhaps his style will emerge in the manner of Picasso or Modigliani—he must be free to explore.

Who knows, maybe he could find fame as a street artist, capturing the likenesses of passers-by and selling the finished articles to pay for those international expeditions.

Fork to fork

In his working life, your guy consumed a frightening quantity of lunchtime sandwiches and sugary snacks. (Sorry, he lied about the salads and crisp, green apples). At home he will have eaten, and possibly cooked, healthy, nutritious meals with plenty of fresh fruit and vegetables, but it is less likely he had the leisure to enjoy providing real food with his own hands. Now he can make up for lost time, by growing his, and your, five servings a day.

Apart from the obvious benefits to the housekeeping and knowing the provenance of your food, growing your own herbs and vegetables provides fresh air, exercise, and a primal satisfaction. All he needs to get started is a packet of seeds and a sunny window lesge with pots or trays to plant them in. Fragrant herbs like parsley, sage, rosemary, and thyme, (yes, do sing along) coriander, basil, chives, and oregano can be grown in a window box and can form the basis of inexpensive and delicious pasta and risotto dishes with just of a dash of olive oil, some garlic, and an onion.

Potatoes can be grown in a dustbin and tomatoes in pots. With more space, low-maintenance, raised beds can deliver beans, peas, carrots, squash, onions, and sweet corn. If you have the space and heart for hens, you can practically live off the land and share your bounty with friends.

Song, Sung Blue

With apologies to Neil Diamond, who at the age of 70 has become cool with the kids and might be a role model for our very own retired songbird. These days you don't have to be Elvis, hanging around Sun Records to record "My Happiness" for your mama's birthday, to be discovered. In the 21st century, he can write, record, and post his own music online, and with the marketing talent or boardroom skills he may have gleaned in his day job, be the next international singing sensation.

"He doesn't read music or play an instrument," you might protest, but a lack of ability presents no obstacle to celebrity. He can download the appropriate accompaniment from the internet, including backing vocals, and find the sound he is looking for with one of many of the music mixing computer programs available (many for free). It's that easy.

Perhaps he likes opera and would like to give a rendition of one of the great arias, or maybe blues is his bag, as no one says anymore. He could rock the house, sing down-home country, or fashion himself the next great retired rapper. He might even surprise you with a love song that he has written himself...not that his love is any surprise to you, who support him no matter how far off-key he might stray.

The Day of the Cryptids

In his lifetime, your chap might think he has seen it all: lions in the Serengeti, elephants in India, even the duck-billed platypus in the Galapagos Islands. Indeed, if he has seen the extraordinarily unlikely duck-billed platypus, he will be one step nearer to his new hobby: the study of cryptozoology. He may have to suspend his disbelief in order to hunt for evidence of cryptids—creatures for whose existence there is no real scientific evidence, such as Bigfoot and the Loch Ness Monster, or the lesser known Beast of Bodmin in England or the Bladinboro in North Carolina. There are hundreds more, from Giant

Squid and Moose-bears, to big cats from
around the world.

Perhaps your man is a wise old bird,
unstrayed by the blurring edges between
provable reality and the mad fantasy world
of mythical creatures which has bamboozled
many of our otherwise sensible youth! Encourage
him to open his mind and take up this new "science."
With his new and interesting young friends, he will be able
to create satisfying charts of "sightings" and scrapbooks
of shaky photographic evidence, even perhaps attending
conventions and conferences in a land far, far away…

Sign here, please

When Retired Man was just a boy, collecting things was all the rage. Every kid had a precious collection of stamps or rocks, records, or picture cards; they gave them away with tea and cigarettes, which adults would pass onto children. (The trinkets, that is. Not the cigarettes.) Just what he collected would have depended on his interests, but odds on he collected something.

Gender stereotype #47: Men love ticking boxes; and many kids were fascinated by collecting autographs of the famous or celebrated in sports or popular music, or stars of stage and screen. He may have forgotten the pleasure of waiting for hours in the rain outside a sport's stadium, for a glimpse of the striker for Manchester United or the pitcher for the Red Sox and the joy of uttering those immortal lines, "Can I have your autograph please?" Why shouldn't he relive those glory days by starting a new autograph collection? He could eschew the obvious rock stars and athletes in favor of politicians or TV weather reporters; the trick is to get them all—and not be accused of stalking!...unless his category is washed-up celebrities flattered by the attention.

> He may have forgotten the pleasure of waiting for hours in the rain outside a sport's stadium, for a glimpse of the striker.

The wheels on the bus go round and round

The arrival of a free bus pass and other forms of subsidized travel has become a mark of achievement for the retired man. Day after day, for years and years, he has poured his hard-earned cash into ticket machines in the daily battle that is commuter travel. He paid top dollar to be squashed in miserably with thousands of others travelling to and from work.

Now that he has reached retirement age, he may be entitled to travel the length and breadth of the country for free. If he makes use of this privilege, for which he has surely paid his dues, he could be away for days at a time. If he undertakes the epic journey from terminus to terminus with only his trusty timetables to guide him, that trek could stretch into weeks, even months, after inevitable cancellations and delays.

He could enjoy the whole of Proust in the time he is away with time enough to spare for *War and Peace*.

He should pack sensibly: warm clothes, wet weather gear, snacks, and drinks, this is not a road trip for the faint-hearted. Why not buy him an eBook reader? He could enjoy the whole of Proust in the time he is away, with time enough to spare for *War and Peace*. You will enjoy enough peaceful solitude to welcome his return. Oh happy, happy day!

Rhyme and reason

When we are young, poetry is a first language; we take in nursery rhymes, lullabies, and rhyming songs in our cradles. Teenage boys write powerful poems, questionable limericks, and boastful football chants, but as they get older men pack away their lyricism with their train sets and toy soldiers (if they pack those away at all.) Today, you must throw down the gauntlet, and get your retiree to arrange and contribute to a poetry reading, at home or in your local bar or pub. Welcome allcomers regardless of age or gender, but to be on the safe side, ask some close friends and family to guarantee their presence. Poems may be any structure—long or short, rhyming or not, original or the work of the greats—but your man must write and read at least one of his own. If he can't find the words let him try haiku, rhyming is not compulsory.

Some cool music like a jazz quartet would help the proceedings, though huge sweaters and tight black trousers, with a jaunty neckerchief are strictly optional.

> Today, you must throw down the gauntlet, and get your retiree to arrange and contribute to a poetry reading.

Go fish!

Fishing is arguably the most popular sport in the world, so it merits a mention here, and let's suppose your guy has never known the joy of hours on a rainy riverbank or buffeting gale-force winds on the high seas.

You could tempt him to try it with the promise of another hat, (by now you should have a hat stand) this one with a jaunty feather and some hand-tied flies hooked in the brim. You could describe the array of equipment he will need; men love gear. Then there are the hours spent tinkering with reels, and practicing the arcane mysteries of tying flies. You could introduce him to the whole new language that he will have to learn to chat with his fishing buddies or remind him that many of the tools on his Swiss Army knife are still, as yet, untried.

You might tease him with tales of the one that got away, and the epic stories of man pitting his wits against an ancient pike, lurking in the depths of a still, blue-green lake. Or simply remind him of how much he enjoys fresh brown trout for supper. But you may need only to paint a picture of the river's peace and tranquility with sunlight playing on the water on a summer's afternoon to find that before long "there's a sign upon the door."

Saturday Night Fever

There are certain dance moves only a man of a certain age can bust. Sadly, not the magnificent posturing of an Argentine goucho smouldering in the tango, or a haughty Prince Charming waltzing his lady around a glittering ballroom, but a mash of flailing arms, gyrating hips, knees together bob, with an occasional Jaggeresque head turn (the pout is optional). Such a man will almost certainly at one time have seen himself rivaling John Travolta's dazzling disco in Saturday Night Fever and he can still do the legendary pointing! Is this your man?

Any teenager will tell you, nothing is quite so embarrassing as this "dad-dancing," and since he has looked after himself, and so boasts the physique of a racing snake, your guy now has every chance to humiliate his grandchildren too, with "granddad-dancing."

Don't wound his feelings with discouragement. Instead, guide him. Dancing is cool, and fantastically good exercise, so why not sign up for classes? You can join in this—you won't even need sequined patent-leather white gloves. At the next family celebration, he could surprise the kids with hip-hop or street dance, as well as a nifty quick step or a romantic fox trot. You could even master the finale of Dirty Dancing together (you know you want to). So dust off those dancing shoes—nobody puts hubby in the corner.

Take in a gig

We all tend to get stuck in a musical groove as we get older, at least as far as popular music is concerned. We have our collections of vinyl, our copies of the same albums on CD, and now, if we have caught up with the technology, the same selection yet again, now downloaded to our MP3 players. Your chap can just about be persuaded to visit an arena to hear Dylan, Cohen, Pink Floyd, the Stones, or Bruce Springsteen (delete as applicable) and convince himself, as he watches the tiny figures strut their stuff from a distance of some miles, that they, like him, have hardly aged at all.

It's time to get him off the sofa or out of the shed and broaden his horizons; he can't spend the next thirty years listening to "(I Can't Get No) Satisfaction" and "The Wall."

First, catch a young person or two, give them a clue as to his taste, and ask them to make him a compilation of some of the new, young bands he is missing and might actually enjoy. Then, bend these same young people

He can't spend the next thirty years listening to "The Wall."

to your will and let him go with them to a live gig or festival to hear them play. Dress code: wellies and waterproofs.

Starry, starry night

Is your man having trouble getting a good night's sleep since he has had to face the prospect of the future after a lifetime of honest toil? Filling his night-time hours as well as those of daylight is your self-appointed task. It is a huge change; so if his colleagues have asked you for ideas for a gift for his retirement, suggest a night telescope and an excellent book on astronomy, so that he can put his change of life into perspective by studying the ever-changing night sky.

The ancient Greeks, the Chinese, the Mayans, and the Indians, undertook detailed and regular observations of the night sky, and early mariners navigated their craft by the position of the stars, so there are splendid precedents for his taking up this study. Astronomy combines many subjects close to the hearts of most men, who pride themselves on their scientific turn of mind.

This subject involves physics, chemistry, meteorology, ontology, cosmology, and some "ologies" that you need an ologologist to explain. When studying the formation and development of the universe there's plenty for him to get his teeth into. As he follows the unfolding of the universe, he can transcribe his findings, like the Great Bear and the Plough, onto splendid charts and pore over them, possibly wearing a velvet smoking jacket and a hat with a tassel. Or at the very least, the nighttime study sessions will put him to sleep.

Fore!

Watch for the telltale signs. Has your man taken to wearing cleats and socks with silly designs? Does he leave the house a symphony in Fair Isle knit with a jaunty cap upon his head and someone else carrying his bags—unless he is auditioning for a part in *Jeeves and Wooster*, he's a goner. They say the only man who doesn't take up golf when he retires is the one who already plays.

You could do worse than give your guy free rein on this one. It gets him out of the house to socialize, amid fresh air and what we shall generously call exercise. If spending three or four hours at your local club is not enough for him (or you), set him the challenge of playing a round on every major golf course in the land.

This will take forward planning, and careful selection. He may have to raise his game to qualify for some courses (this means more practice—hooray!) There are a number of good books and websites for research and when his choices start to include exotic locations, you might consider going along. Mark Twain said "Golf is a good walk spoiled," but for you it could be a good walk with a spa, cocktails at the 19th hole, and a gourmet dinner. For him, it could be the realization of a lifetime ambition, and you get to pack his suitcase because you love him so. After all, he did fold the napkins.

Mark Twain said "Golf is a good walk spoiled," but for you it could be a good walk with a spa, cocktails at the 19th hole, and a gourmet dinner.

Extreme ironing

It is a little known fact that many men, especially those of a certain age, actually enjoy smoothing the crinkles from clean laundry, fresh from the line or tumble dryer, fragrant with the scent of newly-mown grass or fabric conditioner. Perhaps it is because most have not had to do a family load, day-in-day-out, year after year, that it still holds charm and mystery for them. If your man is twiddling his thumbs desolately, show him to the ironing board and give him your faith not to burn the linen. If pressing his shirt collar and cuffs won't hold his interest, introduce him to an aspect of this seemingly domestic chore that will: added danger!

He is happily out of your hair, returning, elated, with a pile of perfectly ironed laundry.

Extreme ironing is an extreme sport and a performance art in which the sportsman takes an ironing board to an extreme location like a raging river, a mountain peak, a motorway, or ski slope and irons items of clothing. The official website describes it thus: "The latest danger sport that combines the thrills of an extreme outdoor activity with the satisfaction of a well-pressed shirt." For you, the helpmeet of the retiree, this is all good news. He is happily out of your hair, returning, elated, with a pile of perfectly ironed laundry.

Music, maestro, please

They call him the music man; he has rhythm oozing from every pore and a melody in his heart. Unfortunately, he has been far too busy earning a living to actually master a musical instrument. In his day, he will tell you, he was forced to memorize his times tables instead and he has never forgotten that incident with a triangle, that marred his percussion career.

But every dog has his day and this is his. There is a full orchestra of instruments from which he can choose, though you may find the drums rough going until he finds his rhythm. Perhaps the time has passed to take up the trumpet, tuba, or the euphonium—they need a lot of puff—but the clarinet or saxophone, the violin, the recorder, or even penny whistle are well within the bounds of possibility. If he learns an orchestral instrument, he could experience the joy of joining an ensemble or amateur orchestra: making music with others is one of the keenest pleasures of learning to play.

If he plumps for a piano, and space does not allow for even a baby grand, a small, electronic keyboard with functions for lots of different instruments might suit him very well. Plus it's not too late for him to fulfill those rock god fantasies by learning the electric guitar. You'll miss him when he is out on the road, but at least you can brag to your lady friends about the rock star you are seeing.

"It was the best of times..."

Your talented Retired Man can no longer claim that lack of time is the only barrier to the great novel he insists is on the tip of his pencil. Accept no more excuses, simply repeat, "Book, now!" whenever he finds an urgent reason to defrost the fridge, rather than getting all those characters out of his head and into the romantic, fantastic, science fictiffic lives he has planned for them. He has been accustomed to making decisions at the office or plant, directing or managing the lives of others, and heaven knows he has seen and heard enough stories unfold in his time. All of these are crucial to weaving the tale of an interesting piece of humanity.

Getting started with a novel is a matter of having a story to tell, and the talent, imagination, organization, and confidence to tell it. The technique can be taught at creative writing classes, either online or on school and college courses. He will learn the differences between plot and character-driven work, and how to develop both. He will learn the vocabulary of the different genres, and why the urbane detective hero might serve his story better if he were an intergalactic space P.I. instead. The key to getting his readers hooked however, is not the denouement of his white-knuckle story, but the opening line—and he will only crack that when he actually gets started...

Whittling

Whittlers do marvelous work, usually in miniature, since they want to be able to carry their work-in-progress with them, in a pocket or bag, to whip out a sharp blade at idle moments. There are no deadlines in whittling; it takes as long as it takes, the antithesis of the fast-paced working world that he has just left. Working

Small birds and animals, boats and toys are the usual choices of the whittler-about-town.

in wood gives immense satisfaction, choosing the right kind for the job, seeing the subject emerge from the piece, then smoothing and finishing the final object. Small birds and animals, boats, and toys are the usual choices of the moden whittler-about-town.

Why should your cool retired guy consider doing it? Well, *Webster's Dictionary* defines it as follows: 1. To cut small bits or pare shavings from a piece of wood. To fashion or shape in this way: whittle a toy boat or other objects. 2. To reduce or eliminate gradually, as if by whittling with a knife. The second definition is surely a metaphor for retirement; gradually eliminating the unnecessary stresses from life, allowing a new and creative life to emerge and. Soon you will be able to look into his empowered eyes and say seductively, "You know how to whittle don't you?"

Sign of the times

Do you have the volume on your television turned up to 40 or more, and shout to each other over the roar? Now could be the time to learn a quieter and more peaceful way to communicate as you grow older, and let's face it, harder of hearing. Quite apart from the ability to swear in front of the grandchildren, signing is a useful and beautiful language to master. It is elegant and expressive and once he has it under his belt, your man could use it to help others.

Perhaps he could offer to sign at local theatrical productions, for the enjoyment of non-hearing audience members. Churches often have choirs for the deaf, who sign along with the congregation. If he becomes fluent, he could assist in the classroom, working one on one with non-hearing children. Or he could do all three, signing *Jesus Christ: Superstar* for religious deaf children. Many adult education schools hold sign classes. A quick Google search will give details of the same in every country.

Like all languages, signing takes practice but at the very least, your man will find it useful in communicating with his dentist. Don't they always strike up riveting conversation when one has a mouthful of cotton wool and sharp pointy instruments?

Go ape!

When your chap's colleagues ask you what kind of a retirement party he may like, or what gift they should give to commemorate the event, don't opt for a glass of tepid wine and some potato chips in the office, culminating in a pen he no longer needs, or an attractive carriage clock. Ask them to spend the office collection on an aerial assault course. And invite his colleagues to join him.

Many aerial assault courses include abseiling, climbing walls, and zip lines. Go Ape specializes in tree top outdoor zip lines, Tarzan swings and obstacles, both in the UK and US. All providers promise that these outdoor adventure activities are properly supervised, with well-maintained equipment and safety harnesses, inspected regularly, as well as on-site instruction. However, as with other adventure activities, it is a good idea for your chap to have a medical check-up to eliminate any health niggles and insurance problems before he swings from branch to branch. Slip the doctor a twenty to exclaim, upon passing muster, that he has never seen such a specimen, and that indeed, your man is fit to wrestle bears.

Younger friends and family members will love this; ask them along and your chap's coolness quotient and confidence will go through the roof. You know your adventurous man—when he can fly through the trees, why on earth should he settle for a stroll in the park?

Avatar

Your man may feel that his life so far, though happy, has not fulfilled the promise of adventure and excitement of which he dreamed in his youth. In the back of his mind, he may think that if only he had been taller; a Norse god called Chad or Brick, with tossing golden curls, rippling muscles, chiseled features and a rugged jaw, he could have made those dreams come true.

It is not too late. He can cut a different profile by creating an avatar on a 3D virtual website like Second Life. Here, Chad can safely present himself as a ruthless property tycoon, romantic poet, or dashing movie star. He can have a whole new career as an entrepreneur, an architect or a lawyer, whatever he chooses. He can live in a palatial home designed by Chad the architect, and enjoy a vivid social life. He might boost his pension too, by making real money and converting Second Life's "Linden dollars" into hard currency in the real world, after he has made his pile in retail.

Click on Second Life's website to see a tutorial on how to create an avatar, navigate the world, socialize and make money. Who knows: Chad might fall in love with Mimi, that raven-haired minx of yours, and you could live happily ever after in both worlds.

Meeting and greeting

He has retired, and your chap can see that the trouble with going to work everyday is that he doesn't seem to know anybody in his own neighbourhood anymore. Or perhaps you have downsized recently or moved closer to your grandchildren and neither of you has had an opportunity to make new friends. In any event, it is time to get out there and find some kindred spirits.

You, of course are frantically busy, so challenge him to get to know at least three new people who live in your building, on your block or street, before the month is out. This is no suggestion he lurk at their doors with damp palms and a forward grin, waiting to pounce. There are civilized ways to get acquainted. There may be a local residents' association to join, or a club or society that reflects his hobbies or interests, like music or film, board games, or even fantasy role play (ah, the timeless fascination of Dungeons & Dragons). The only rule is it that it must be within walking distance. He could join a sports club—badminton, squash or golf, table tennis or tiddlywinks, or a poker school, it doesn't matter what.

Alternatively, he could earn the gratitude of all the neighbours by booking a venue and inviting them to join in a version of speed dating, without the pairing off, so that everyone can get to know one another. Or host a neighbourhood barbecue.

Honeybee, honeybee, buzz if you like me

In spring an old man's fancy turns to beekeeping so that in winter it may turn to honey. Picture the scene: flames crackle in the grate, a kettle sings upon the oven, and a pile of hot-buttered toast calls to you. With the aid of a stick-with-pine-cone-looking thing on that only people in commercials seem to own, you drizzle your very own heather-scented honey on the topmost slice. This idyll can be yours, if only you persuade Retired Man to take up beekeeping. Better still, he can harvest royal jelly and beeswax, to make superb polish. You (and the bees) will be in clover.

He can start in a small way with good courses online and research national beekeeping associations for information on the best bees and how to keep them. Here's a tip: don't raise killer bees. For starters they make no honey. Honeybees' numbers are diminishing and rely on "hobby" beekeepers' to improve their chances. He will add to the gaiety of his wardrobe with a fetching suit and mask and the veil will disguise his fine lines and wrinkles. Town dwellers, check out urban beekeeping and if you don't like honey suggest he support Bees Abroad, promoting apiculture in developing countries.

Bounce back

Quiet pursuits do not suit every man and yours may be very fit, with a keen sense of adventure. He may not get many opportunities to live life on the edge anymore and this can make him glassy-eyed and listless, with a dull coat.

If you want to put the spring back into his step, suggest he live dangerously. A quick check-up with the doctor (to make sure his heart—and yours—can take it) and there should be no obstacle to a few daredevil activities.

Bungee jumping, especially when sponsored for charity, can be fantastically exhilarating and fulfilling. *Do*: find a reputable company with an impeccable safety record. *Don't*: just join some rubber bands

Remember, if you love him, let him go; if he is yours he will come back to you, if he doesn't, someone forgot "left over right, right over left."

together and tie a granny knot to the nearest bridge, unless your life insurance is fully paid up. Remember, if you love him, let him go; if he is yours he will come back to you, if he doesn't, someone forgot "left over right, right over left."

Seriously, skydiving, whitewater rafting, kayaking, and even windsurfing can all be enjoyed well into old age, provided you take sensible safety precautions. Arrange for friends and family to watch on the big day, and get someone to film the whole thing so that you can feel your heart stop, over and over again.

A toe in the water

Do you recognize this man? He's stout, no longer in the first flush of youth, his trousers rolled up to the knee, a handkerchief knotted at its corners on his head, to protect his balding pate from the sun; he's paddling in the waves at a seaside resort. Of course you don't, unless you are familiar with early 20th-century British saucy postcard art. Your ripped, retired chap in no way matches this description. He has a full head of hair, uses SPF 50, and it is years since he took off his shoes and socks to feel the azure waters of an unknown sea rippling over his feet.

Why not change this and plan a coast-to-coast trip, starting and ending this journey at ocean's edge? The journey can be taken by train, bus, car, or roller skates. This is not an attempt to lure him on an expensive journey; this is an adventure. The aim is to stop and look at the places he passes through, experience what they have to offer, dip a toe in the waters of each culture. If he lives in the interior of one of the vaster continents it may involve plane travel, and real toe-dipping may be omitted if ice floes are present.

And it's a new world record

The medieval philosopher Thomas Aquinas spent his time contemplating how many angels could dance on the head of a pin. In 21st-century Britain, Kam Ma had 1015 metal rings skewered through his body, to break his own world record.

If your chap is bored and restless, wandering from room to room, whistling through his teeth in an annoying fashion, why not suggest that he direct some of that energy into similarly breaking or setting a crazy new world record in something?

He could try to beat the USA's Joel Waul and his world's largest rubber band ball, or gather together some friends to beat the most people dressed as a Smurf (1,253 by the Muckno Mania Festival in Ireland). He could grow the longest fingernails on both hands, the longest beard, or the biggest tomato with the discernible face of Mother Teresa. He might see how many eggs he could break on his own head or stuff into his own mouth, or attempt to qualify as the world's least (or most) hairy man. Perhaps he could consume his own weight in flying saucer candy or shoot lightning bolts from his fingertips. Who knows? The world of records is bizarre; the biggest, smallest, fastest, and slowest, most, and least of whatever takes his fancy could all qualify. Whatever he chooses, though, perhaps you could suggest that he does it at someone else's house?

Making history

We all want to be remembered in history, some of us become the movers and shakers who make it: the Napoleons and Lincolns, the Curies and Pasteurs, Aristotles and Einsteins: an endless and varied list. The rest of us must be content as tellers of tales, keepers of the exploits and achievements of heroes of the human story. The old masters used sculpture and painting to illustrate these tales. Your Retired Man may have to be more inventive so that, in a flash, he can fashion great moments in history from everyday materials. For example, the wedding of Prince William and his bride was knitted recently, losing none of the majesty or spectacle.

Pipe cleaners, pencils and cork, cardboard and glue, even the humble handkerchief can be pressed into service to entertain and educate the young with his version of Great Moments in History. Twist coloured pipe cleaners to demonstrate the double helix! White gloves (of course you have some) and magic markers make great finger puppets when throngs are called for—angry mobs, choirs of angels, and so on. An assorted pack of coloured felt is very handy and hobby stores sell dolly wigs for beards and hair, although trusty wool works well. Start small (perhaps The War of 1812) and build up (The War of 1813: The Empire Strikes Back). Soon he will be able to re-enact the great battles of history, the love stories of our time, and the timeless, mighty myths and legends on the fingers of one hand!

Let's go fly a kite

The summer breeze is blowing the long grass across the meadow.
The waves break on the beach with white horses as far as the
eye can see. Describe these scenes to Retired Man and he will be
transported instantly to his childhood days when, if he was any
kind of a boy, he will certainly have made and flown his own kite.

Now he has time on his hands and unlimited access to sticks, paper,
twine, and glue, and his very own paint box or crayons, he could
amuse himself by making a kite again, to fly by himself or with
his grandchildren. He could even pass on the wisdom and secrets
of kite- making to the next generation. A kite does not have to be
fancy to fly, and the flying is what it is all about. A simple
diamond or box kite is easy to make and instructions
can be downloaded from the internet.

He could go to town, and buy silk instead of paper, or
decorate the tail with ribbons, but he should have a
few test runs before he gets carried away. When he
has got the hang of it, he might join a kite-flying
club, chasing the wind to find the optimum
flying conditions. It's a simple enough
pleasure to recapture the magic of a
scrap of paper dipping and coursing in
the blue sky. He may, however, have to re-learn
how to run backwards without falling over.

It's movie night

In these days of big, blockbuster movies and multiplex cinemas, it is hard to remember that when your retiree was a boy, many children started their weekends off at Saturday morning picture club. The keynote here was variety. There might be a cartoon, a cliffhanger serial, a western, or a gangster flick, a sing-a-long musical and a travel documentary all on the same bill. Even the adults enjoyed a double feature—a "B" movie before the main film—in the afternoon or evening. Many of those "B" movies are cult classics.

The next time that he complains that there is nothing on television and that the multiplex cinema in town is showing the same "action" or fantasy movie in each, suggest that he hosts his own movie marathon night, with all the variety and interest of his heyday. It is possible to hire prints or DVDs from the distributers for public broadcast and he could plan a night just like the good old days, maybe calling it something witty like "Déja Vu" and advertise locally, donating the modest proceeds to charity.

If his small local cinema or theatre is "dark," he might be able to hire it. An outdoor show on the beach, or in the grounds of a local historical building, would be great in the summer. Start with cartoons for the children and move on to some great "B" movies and finish with a classic. Fantastic!

Poker Face

Did your chap stare blankly at you over coffee this morning? You have no idea what he may be thinking, and he's not telling. He may a little bored or distracted—after all he's not used to relaxing! That's a pretty effective poker face he is showing to the world, so why not suggest that he puts it to good use? His face could be his fortune. Let him learn poker; he can get the basics from a dozen Internet sites, and you could get him some of those cool, expandable armbands to hold up his shirtsleeves and a nice green eyeshade. It may prove useful if he's ever entangled in a web of international intrigue. If he gets very good, he could start a poker school (or his own global conspiracy...) There are two ways to win a poker hand, and therefore the 'pot', which is the total of bets made. The first is to have the highest-ranking hand: the lower the odds of getting the hand, the stronger it ranks.

Poker may prove useful if he's ever entangled in a web of international intrigue.

The other is where your guy's special talent comes in: to bluff the other players into thinking he has a stronger hand, so that they "fold," giving up and allowing him to take the pot. With his poker face, that'll be easy. He could make a matchstick model of Notre Dame with his winnings. If he burns through his fortune, you'll get a spectacle. (Editor's note: In all seriousness, retired couples, do not play with fire unless you have a child supervising you.)

That man's got talent

O r has he? Settle the matter once and for all, and get him out of the house by suggesting that he audition for a TV talent show. Unless you have been visiting friends on another planet or hibernating in a deep cave, you've probably noticed that they are very popular viewing at the moment. (But if you did either of those things, you would perfect for the variety show, astronaut bear! Your stage name will be Major Ursa.)

Every series discovers some untrained, sensational new talent who shoots to international stardom and a season on a cruise ship. Of course, for every superstar, they film a thousand terrible turns just to satisfy the bloodlust of the baying live audience.

So think carefully before you wave him off, with his dancing dog, his bagpipes, his tap shoes, and all his dreams tied up in a spotted handkerchief. Ask yourself, 'Has my man got what it takes, or will he return to me after days in line under a cold rain just to get an audition, a broken man—his hopes shattered and his journey at an end? Or worse, could he end up in an outtake show, utterly humiliated; one of those terrible acts that don't even make it to the live show? Or even worse still, he could win the series and be forced to sail on a cruise ship? Go on, it's worth the risk! Now let's take that one more time from the top: "Start spreading the news…"

Fabulous baker boy

If you do not live near to an Artisan bakery, or French Patisserie, then you may want to paint a small pencil moustache on your man's upper lip, and encourage him to roll up his sleeves and bake!

Fresh, home-baked bread is delicious and nutritious, and comes in endless varieties. The principle is exactly the same whatever kind of loaf you bake. The flour needs to be mixed with liquid and a raising agent (yeast) until it forms a ball. Then, like the rest of us, it needs to be kneaded (that's the therapeutic part) until it is soft and elastic, and left to rest in

When it has doubled in size (so like real life) the dough is kneaded again and left to rise once more.

a warm place. When it has doubled in size (again, so like real life) it is kneaded again and left to rise once more. The dough is then baked until golden brown. Your retiree will love doing this; all his hard work is rewarded with one of life's truly great pleasures—fresh bread! Encourage him to move on to croissants and pastries, tarts and flans. Your kitchen will always smell delicious and buyers will flock to your door should you be thinking of downsizing!

The book group

There was a time when the only opportunity that poor, Retired Man had to lose himself in the pages of the latest No. 1 best-seller was on the beach, during his annual holiday. He sometimes managed a line or two in a title someone had recommended, only to fall asleep, nose in spine. Now, he has the time, but the labyrinthine shelves of possibilities are too bewildering.

He needs guidance from like-minded people, who know what's what. The answer is to join or set up his own book group. A literary society's vitality stems from that same sea of options about which book to read; Jim wants to open *Crime and Punishment* while George recommends *The Da Vinci Code*. Patrick is all for *Love in the Time of Cholera* and David insists on Jumpers. So, they'll have a few beers, discuss the pros and cons and decide on the latest Stephen King novel.

A week or two later, they'll meet (over more beers) to discuss the characterization, plot, and subtext, and choose the next book. He'll have a good time, catch up on the latest stock prices (men don't gossip, apparently—no, really) and he'll build up an eclectic library. Dress code is casual, but pants are recommended.

Soft hands, smooth feet

He owns a pair of nail clippers and a metal file and can be trusted to make brisk use of a soapy nailbrush, but he thinks "cuticle" is a term of endearment. He looks mistrustfully upon the manicure, associating it with dubiously-aquired wealth and a life unencumbered by manual work. Looking after his hands is both a gender and a class issue for your chap.

He need not suffer for hygiene, but if you want your guy to take care of his hands, you'll have to put the "man" back into manicure. Don't tease him by suggesting he wear nail polish, and do offer straightforward tips.

If you want your guy to take care of his hands, you'll have to put the "man" back into manicure.

Teach him to soak his fingertips for five minutes to make trimming the nails easier, after scrubbing and before shaping lightly with an emery board. Show him buffing (you'll need to explain it's not naked manicuring but increases healthy blood flow) and demonstrate how to use a drop of cuticle oil on each nail to stop them drying out. Massage a good quality, scent-free hand cream into his knuckles, explaining a hand massage can ease joint pains and stiffness. Now for the feet, how do you put the "ped" back into pedicure...? Pay a child to slough layers from his heels? No, it won't do. He can learn to do it himself.

Take a gap year

Young people, it seems, are now entitled to take a year out of their busy schedule, usually between school and University, or college and getting a job, in which to meet interesting people, see the world, and experience "life." Referred to as "my gap year," this is now a worldwide phenomenon and not confined to the youth population. You and your retired man deserve the same chance to travel the world on an economy ticket, and backpack the trails around Thailand and Laos, Australia and China as the youth of today. (Not to mention meet all your friends from back home, drink cheap beer, and fail to see much of the countries you visit.)

You could probably do it more comfortably of course, but where is your sense of adventure? Lighten up, dig out that backpack, and jump on a plane. Or you could find some other way to spend a year before settling down to wait for senility. Travel really does broaden the mind, but perhaps you and your guy could theme your trip to enjoy something you already you know you love. A food-themed year perhaps—eat your way around the world, or see opera in every famous opera house. Perhaps art is your thing, or archeology, or even UFO spotting? Try lending your skills along the way; dig wells in Africa, build a school in South America, or teach an Italian politician to lie. Whatever you do, you'll learn some essential life skills that were lacking from the boardroom!

God only knows

Retired man is in good voice, singing his heart out in the shower, improvising with the shampoo for a microphone. His repertoire may be limited; but keen as he is on the Beach Boys, he attempts all the voices simultaneously in the complex parts, and there's no doubt he's badly let down by his imaginary band in the close harmonies. To fulfill his musical dreams in the real world he must put on a striped blazer and a straw boater and find some real friends to sing with. Apparently, anyone can learn to sing and singing—especially with others in a choir or barbershop quartet—is extremely good for your health, resulting in a euphoria after a good rehearsal or performance that

> To fulfill his musical dreams he must put on a striped blazer and a straw boater and find some real friends to sing with.

can last for days. The last time your man joined such a group was when the entire world gathered to buy itself a Coca-Cola.

Luckily, choirs are springing up all over the place, like Toadstools after the Rain, and other poorly named choirs out there. This new spate of chanteuring attracts singers, young and old, in their thousands. Look for ads in local newspapers and on websites calling for singers to audition and send your chap along. Make sure he understands not to fall for any casting couch tactics.

Blog blog blog

In the 21st century, the whole world blogs about everything from Aardvarks to Zoroastrianism (most notably at Zoroastrianism-ForAardvarks.com). Has your guy got some special interest to fascinate countless others with? Has he had a particularly dramatic life, or even one filled with subtler insights into the emotional aspects of drying paint? Blogs present a personal viewpoint on interests like food or travel or the blogger's innermost thoughts. Think of it as an online journal with attitude, like pre-Internet diaries, marked "Strictly Private", penned in the hope that others would breach them. You'll be surprised what strikes a chord with readers.

The novice blogger can set up a blog for free in five minutes. Most blogging sites will automatically offer his work to search engines based on keywords he selects to describe the blog, and also based on content. He will need to write and update an entry on his chosen subject on a regular, if not daily basis. It can help to illustrate text with uploaded images. You will be able to assess the level of interest from Cyberville by the number of 'hits' on his site.

So, if RM writes cogently and has something to say, blogging could be for him. Now, for a subject, how about he takes up every challenge in this book and blogs about his experiences?

Tombstone blues

How often have you and your chap passed by a graveyard, churchyard, or cemetery without a backward glance? Perhaps you whistle as you pass, showing the Grim Reaper that you don't have time for his nonsense with decades in you yet! And so you do. But if your man gets the blues from time to time (and which of us doesn't when he imagines old Grim to be close at hand) help him face his fears by reading tombstone epitaphs.

He can make a proper hobby of this, travelling the world, spotting the graves of the famous, but for the time being, take a look at the tombstones of ordinary folk. He could spend long winter evenings writing his own epitaph. Some witty and inspiring examples:

Here lies the body of Detlof Swenson. Waiter.
God finally caught his eye.

Here lies the body of our Anna
Done to death by a banana
It wasn't the fruit that laid her low
But the skin of the thing that made her go.

Rebecca Freeland 1741
She drank good ale,
good punch and wine
And lived to the age of 99.

REBECCA
FREELAND
1741

SHE DRANK GOOD ALE,
GOOD PUNCH AND WINE
AND LIVED TO THE AGE OF 99.

Tree walking

Has your chap developed a tendency to gloom when he contemplates the passing years? If your cheery reminders that there is "life in the old dog yet" seem only to scour his nerves just like his new-found grumpiness gets on yours, it's time you both found your nearest ancient forest and spent some time with the trees.

In the USA you have the breadth of a continent which is home to California sequoia (giant redwood) and the pine forests of Maine to explore; The US National Parks Service is your best recourse. In Australia, you have a unique rainforest ecosystem to visit; if his grumps are particularly resolute, take a trip further afield. The National Trust looks after much of the ancient forests of Britain, like the gnarled chestnut walk and 1000-year-old Otway Oak at Croft Castle in Herefordshire. Then there's the rest of the world.

It is literally "awesome" to be in the presence of ancient trees—their silent parliament giving, as it does, a sense of history's span and the many human lifetimes lived beneath their branches. The wildlife is outstanding too. It rather puts our allotted three-score and ten into perspective. So with a rousing rendition of "You are Sixty, Going on Seventy" (with apologies to The Sound of the Music), and a bright smile, head for the trees.

We all scream for ice cream

Once upon a time, when the world was young and your guy was in short pants, the sky grew dark. A cloud of cold fog descended and people forgot that once, real ice cream came in many delicious varieties. It is hard to imagine in a post-Ben & Jerry's world, that for a brief period, everything was in either vanilla, chocolate, or tutti-frutti.

But the ice cream fairy waved her wand, and people remembered that ice cream could be made with real cream, in delicious, natural flavours, like peach and cherry, salted caramel, and cinnamon. Then some bright spark invented the domestic ice cream maker and hey presto! We could all indulge our wildest ice cream fantasies at home. Sadly, no one has told Retired Man this, and he is still a slave to what's on sale at the supermarket freezer.

Buy an ice cream maker, download a basic recipe and let him tease his taste buds by inventing his own unique ice cream flavour. If he goes it alone, he might invent something wild, like strawberry and black pepper, or butternut squash with fig, or he could buy seasonal fresh fruits and blend an exquisite sorbet. He might even get a cart and a tinkling tune and take to the streets. What a thought...

Life is a rollercoaster

Life is all about the ups and downs, the adrenaline rushes and the fight-or-flight response. We are designed for excitement. During a busy working life, the dips and peaks tend toward kids, finances and personal relationships.

> There's something about the slow crawl up the steep slope, the eternal pause at the apex and the screaming, stomach-churning drop into infinity.

Retired Man is no slouch when it comes to dealing with danger. He would face a roaring lion or an angry emu to protect his family, if such courage were called for, but he may not be a great thrill-seeker.

Rock his world by planning and executing a tour of the best rollercoaster and thrill rides he can visit in a fortnight. Not that we don't love the new machines that flip, spin, and seek out new axes on which to rotate the rider, but there's something about the slow crawl up the steep slope, the eternal pause at the apex and the screaming, stomach-churning drop into infinity that draws us close to the rollercoaster in old age. Perhaps it's its similarity to everyday life back when the children were just learning to walk. Of course, like having children, it is not recommended to those with a weak heart so check with your doctor before you go.

Vinyl solution

Are your shelves stacked with priceless vinyl albums, each with its memory of the time and place where he first heard it etched into the grooves or inked in coffee and cigarette stains on the sleeves? Some even have his name written on the middle of the disc to prevent party pilfering.

It's a fair bet that you have another set of shelves or a rack on the wall, creaking under the weight of a set of duplicate CDs. This music collection is the history of popular music from the '50s to the present made plastic. He's hip these days, downloading music to his tablet or smartphone. The vast stack of records gathering dust and taking up valuable space must earn its keep! What he needs is a turntable that converts albums to digital music tracks, and months to luxuriate in the pleasure of wallowing in the emotion of every track, while reliving every precious moment of his youth.

He can scan the sleeves as well—coffee stains and all—to save his memories of friends (and girlfriends) past. As he pulls each cherished disc off the rotor, sliding it in its garments for the last time, he can list it for sale or auction online, knowing it will go to a loving collector who will treat it right. As an added touch, suggest he use the proceeds to procure tickets to the legendary artist who produced the album (or tribute artist if this is no longer possible).

Vroom, vroom

Oh, what dust clouds I shall make!
What carts I shall fling into the ditch!
Mr. Toad

What fellow cannot empathize with the sentiments of Kenneth Graeme's notorious yet endearing Toad of Toad Hall, anticipating the open road in his new motor? Whatever the psychological significance, a yearning to get behind the wheel of a flashy high-performance car is high on many men's bucket list.

Porsche. Ferrari, Lamborghini, or Aston Martin...sadly these "dream" cars are way beyond the depth of most people's pockets. Yet all is not lost! It is still possible to give your man the sheer power and magnificent craftsmanship of the world's most desirable cars, if only for a few hours. Many racetracks organize race day packages, where, for a fee, your guy can drive around the circuit at very high speeds, albeit under controlled circumstances, with supervision, and with all the safety measures in place.

This treat doesn't come cheap, but isn't it worth it to see his little face light up? This is something every man with petrol in his veins should experience once. When the drone of the engine is just a memory in the drone of his voice, you can tune out the descriptions of cam shafts and fuel injection, knowing you have done your spousal duty to make him happy.

A friend indeed

When economic times are hard, the hospitals and hospices, where all this birth and bone-setting are happening often find resources severely stretched.

Dedicated doctors, nurses, and other professionals are on the front-line, and now that retired man has a little more time he should volunteer at these vital institutions. There are a variety of important roles for "friends" to perform. He could lend his imagination and organizational skills to planning community fundraisers for the hospital: picnics and rummage sales, sponsor races, charitable dinners, and auctions. As well as raising money, these events draw the community together.

He could help out with transport between outpatient or outreach clinics, or visit and read to lonely patients. If he has a kind face— he could put it to good use explaining things to the bewildered elderly and if he is a linguist, translate for foreigners who might be frightened and vulnerable. There are laughs a-plenty even when times are grim, and no one needs your man's renowned humour more than the sick and suffering. He could even share his famous "Doctor, Doctor" jokes, when the staff is out of earshot.

Grow a mo!

At this stage in his life, your man may have the body of a 40-year-old, and the razor sharp mind of a man half his age, but it is possible that he is facing a hirsute challenge, and he may well be sensitive about this. Direct his attention away from the top of his head and remind him that if he puts away his razor, he is still fully in control of his beard and mustache.

There are many styles from which to choose: from the goatee beard and Zapata mustache, (probably best avoided) to the RAF handlebar and full sea captain. In between lie the toothbrush and pencil, Fu Man Chu, and designer stubble. Take him to your local joke store to buy mustaches or false beards, sto try out a variety of styles in the privacy of his own home. When he has found one he likes, encourage him to go into full production.

He could be helping others while he gives himself a confidence boost, by cashing in on the growing trend to gain sponsorship to sport mustaches for charity, and the chance to shave them off. The month of November, has even been renamed Movember since 2004, when a charity raises both worldwide awareness of Prostate cancer and money for research. This November let him adopt their slogan, "Grow a mo!" going all out to get sponsored.

Bearding the Bard

F ew of us reach our sixties without at least nodding off to the mighty works of William Shakespeare. If your retiree is now sidling out of the room muttering about urgent whittling, he may still bear the literal scars of that mishap, when as a schoolboy he tripped carrying a spear in *Julius Caesar*. Perhaps the damage is less obvious, like the trauma of donning tights and a wig to muddle through the role of

> Ease his rattled nerves with a pleasurable yet intensive course in the *Complete Works* of Shakespeare.

Mustardseed in *A Midsummer Night's Dream*. Lure him back into the room by setting out a large scotch. Shut the door behind him, and ease his rattled nerves with a pleasurable yet intensive course in the *Complete Works of Shakespeare*.

So here's the plan: watch, read, or otherwise experience every one of Shakespeare's plays over the next twelve months. Traditional theatre is not the first consideration. If you can only get to see *Richard the Third on Ice*, or *The Merchant of Venice* performed by lip-synching poodles at the pet shop's Christmas show, enjoy watching Frou-Frou as a memorable Shylock. Any Shakespeare performance counts, even Hamlet performed by mime artists on unicycles in a multi-story car park, provided that he stays till the curtain (or barrier) comes down.

This is so unexpected

In awards season, we can't turn on the TV or open a newspaper without being asked to swoon over red carpet gowns or invoke outrage at celebrities' antics. We weep with the winners during their acceptance speeches and empathize with the losers putting a brave face on their own disappointment. Some speeches are brilliantly witty and thankfully brief, some rambling and emotional, but all have more thanks than there is time for.

Your grateful and emotional guy may have a few "thank yous" of his own as he retires, after enjoying decades of love and support from friends and family, and no way to express them. Why not hold your own awards ceremony, with red carpet, killer evening wear, and awards categories like Best Lunch-Maker, Best Supporting Commuter, Best Daughter and/or

Edit together some home movies and coach him so that he has a terrific speech prepared.

Son (make sure that all siblings receive equal recognition, so no best supporting child), Best Cameraman (for all those holiday snaps), and the role for which you must surely be a shoe in, Best Supporting Actress Dragged on a "Fun" Vacation (Fishing). He gets a lifetime achievement award and guests can offer glowing tributes. Edit together some home movies to illustrate the point, and coach him so that he has a terrific speech prepared. "This is so unexpected..."

Be his own Banksy

In our lifetime, graffiti has been elevated from mere vandalism to an art form. Well, not all street art. The tags littering the walls of our urban environment do have something to say—if only, "I exist," or "It's not fair," but art like that of the famous Banksy began as guerilla graffiti, yet now commands big bucks in galleries too.

Your chap, now that he has retired, may feel that at last he has the time to explore his own artistic side. Discouraged in his youth by the confines of technique, he felt he couldn't master the mixing of colours and delicate brushwork needed for watercolour. Don't smother his self-expression with a paint-by-numbers kit. Buy him some spray cans, a hoodie, and facemask, and set him loose. That being said, he may want to map out his ideas on squared paper first and transfer it to a chalk grid on (his own) garage wall. Then, when he's ready, he can start vandalizing the neighbour's garage.

His vision could exhibit the existential angst and alienation he feels in retirement...or it could be a nice picture of some cows.

The list

Has Retired Man's book group fallen apart? That can happen; people move away, or find the commitment too much. Sometimes personalities clash, or Mr Intellectual keeps choosing 400-page tomes in the original Urdu. Or maybe the snacks were stale. Whatever the reason, its demise has left your chap wandering around the bookstore like a lost soul.

Let's assume RM has real friends of all ages, many backgrounds, and both genders. Ask them to recommend books to him that they find interesting, stimulating, and engaging. In turn, he will do the same for them. This is a terrific way to get a wide and varied wish-list of titles from people with things in common.

Mutual discoveries like this can add depth to casual friendships, although, of course there is the risk that they could hold some worrying surprises too.

It can also reveal a great deal about the interests of his friends and how they see him. Mutual discoveries like this can add depth to casual friendships, although, of course there is the risk that they could hold some worrying surprises too. But who knows? Your man may find himself quite taken with the recommended *Anarchist Cookbook.*

Dig deep

If there are four words that send a chill into the hearts of strong men, they are fund-raiser and black tie. Not that your guy is mean, but the annual social events arranged to persuade guests to dig deep in their pockets for good causes are monotonously similar: same food, same band, same tables, same old, same old.

Inspire him to be the change he wants to see in the charitable world by organizing something different this year. How about inviting circus performers to attend and teach the diners some simple skills, or take over a local theatre or cinema and let the guests hold a talent show? Perhaps he could make each table a quiz team, and host a general quiz with an unusual prize? If an auction is needed, why not make the lots all edible, or commission artwork by the guests, instead of the usual fruit baskets, spa days, and dinners for two? Remember "Grow a Mo"? (see page 79) Why not get all male guests to bring their mustaches to the party next November, or charge for entry into a best beard contest? It's time for him to get his thinking cap on.

Oh and black tie? Why not make this year's event red tie or polka dot, kipper, bootlace, or bolero…cummerbunds optional?

Cultivation, cultivation, cultivation

One of the greatest pleasures for the green-fingered retiree is the graduation from weekend gardener to horticulturist. If your chap has the DNA of a botanist and the creative aspirations of a god, he should cultivate his own hybrid flower. Each species has its own specific requirements, but the general principles and equipment are the same. When he is successful, he can be immortalized— or better, immortalize you—in the annals of botany by naming and registering a hybrid.

Hybridization requires basic knowledge of his chosen plant's anatomy (he must know his stigmas from his styles, his sepals from his anthers). The terminology can be confusing, but the parent plants are generally female: pod parent with stigma, and male: seed parent with stamens. Observing the flower's peak times for pollination, he will then emasculate the male with some nifty scissor work too disturbing to discuss. That done, he pollinates her with the aid of a soft brush. No license required.

Be patient; he may create many stunning and exciting new varieties, but will also know the sorrow of failure. Have a gin and tonic at the ready.

Om...

In the first days of retirement, it can be almost impossible to relax and transition from work to a slower pace. His brain has been programmed to solve problems, make decisions, and complete tasks. He will find plenty of occasions to use those skills in retirement, but might need to find a new way to rest and relax.

Meditation does not demand that you sell up and move to an Ashram, or that he cast himself at the feet of a Maharishi or a Bhagwan. There is absolutely no need, or indeed excuse, for an orange kaftan or any head-shaving, and you should positively discourage hanging about in airports, harassing travellers with volumes of incomprehensible treatises on the meaning of life.

Simple meditation is a useful relaxation technique, involving nothing more complicated than a quiet, dim space, breathing techniques, and a mantra or phrase he repeats to focus his mind. Looking into a candle flame can help with bringing his concentration back to emptiness when it wanders. Like all good things, meditation takes practice to perfect. Fortunately, patience is one of the virtues he seeks to inculcate. Once mastered, he will be able to do it anywhere, in the dentist's chair, on the bus, and when accosted by chanting youths in orange robes...

There is absolutely no need, or indeed excuse, for an orange kaftan or any head-shaving.

In the wilderness

If you went out of town tomorrow and left your man home alone for a week, would he survive? Could he forage in the fridge, light the stove, and feed himself? Could he build a shelter (or make the bed, as we call it)? If the answer to these questions is "Yes, of course," then your retired guy is definitely ready for something a little more challenging.

Do you remember camping out as a child? You pitched a tent, built a fire, caught and cooked your supper (or scorched the sausages and beans your mother packed if you didn't trust that less-dependable Mother Nature to provide)?

How long is it since your man lived off the land, armed only with a penknife?

How long is it since your man lived off the land, armed only with a penknife, his keen intelligence and the *Boy's Own Book of Survival*? It is a man's natural instinct after all.

Wilderness is hard to define, but a little research will show where the nearest "wilderness" lies. Your man may learn how to eat insects and filter water through sand, charcoal, and grass in his own socks, or enjoy more of a safari with log cabins and all modern conveniences, but the important thing is to reconnect with nature in all its forms: owls hooting, bears growling and the lonesome cry of the elk.

E-publish and be damned

Your retired chap has taken the advice on page 44 and finally completed his novel. This is a fantastic achievement of which he should be justifiably proud. In his creative writing course, he met other accomplished novelists. Friends agree that these works deserve to be published. Unfortunately, while over half a million English-language books are published each year, millions more are propping up the coffee table leg of their author's home.

The point is, it is extremely difficult to get new work read, let alone accepted for publication. Let this be his challenge: to publish himself online. He and his fellow authors can publish through a website of their own and build up a readership with readers online. If this is successful, a publisher may pick up the book to publish in the traditional market. There is software available online to allow people to read sample pages and download in e-book form and he can market it through social networking sites like Facebook. He can also get physical copies printed via online printers.

He should just follow a few basic rules. If possible, get a profesional editor to read and correct any inconsistancies in the work, and be very, very careful not to infringe anyone's copyrighted work (while protecting his own!). He must also be sure not to libel anyone; he could be prosecuted. Finally, don't call it *Parry Hotter* or *The Michelangelo Code* though you could probably write a great book called *Parry Hotter and The Michelangelo Code*.

Next top model

It is very likely that in his boyhood, your man spent many a happy hour with tiny pieces of plastic and a tube of glue, building scale-model aircraft like the Lancaster and the Halifax, the Spitfire, and the Focke-wolf. (If you want to humour him, know that the Lancaster was superior to the Halifax in bomb-loading and altitude.) He would then have carefully painted the models with little pots of enamel paint that smelled marvellous.

If it wasn't aircraft, he made racecars or a stations, farms, and trees—a landscape for a model railway. Now is the time to dust off his model-making skills. There are dozens of kits available: shops, vintage and racing cars, planes, boats, and trains, stately homes, and castles. He could try other materials and methods now that he is grown up. Matchstick models of great

Beware if he sits at the table feverishly constructing mountains from mashed potato.

cathedrals of the world are popular, (no, really), he could make papier-mâché masks for Halloween, or contribute to grandchildren's school projects.

Beware if he sits at the table feverishly constructing mountains from mashed potato, though. It's time to hide the DVD of *Close Encounters of the Third Kind*.

Hula-Hooping

Men and women of a certain age will remember the great crazes of the late 1950s, the yo-yo, and the hula-hoop. The latter may conjure images in RM's mind of girls with shiny hair in bunches and shirts tied beneath the bust. Midriffs dared bared atop white shorts and sneakers, twirling colourful plastic tubes around their middles in marathon sessions. Yo-yos on the hand may not.

In fact, hula-hoops have been known throughout history, but nothing matched the popularity of the Wham-O toy company's plastic hoop in 1957. Yo-yos conjure images of the Smothers Brothers, who are funny and subversive, but don't look good with their shirts tied off. Renewing the fad, your man may retitle it hooping or hoopdance, but if he wants to be bang up-to-date, that faded yellow hoop from the attic won't do. Modern, heavier, larger hoops are used for slow-hooping and body tricks; lighter, thinner tubes work for quick hand tricks.

He could invest in an LED version for hooping after dark. When proficient, he could join in International World Hoop Day. Every year, hoopers dance in every city and country to raise money and donate hoops to others who can't afford them. The hula-hoop is for everyone, except perhaps for those who have recently undergone a hip replacement. Yo-yos, on the other hand…

Your usual, Sir?

Back in the day people worked and lived in the same locale and everyone knew each other, everyone belonged. (Think Bedford Falls in *It's a Wonderful Life*.) But take off those rose-tinted glasses, (free with *Hindsight* magazine) for a moment and look about your own town. Does your retiree feel he is back where he belongs? If the answer is "Not really," it is time to reintegrate him back into the community. His goal is to engineer at least three situations in which someone will utter the immortal words, "Your usual, Sir?"

> His goal is to engineer at least three situations in which someone will utter the immortal words, "Your usual, Sir?"

Then, and only then, will he know that he has come home.

He will frequent the classic barbershop (no man visits a hairstylist), bars, and coffee shops of the town. Each carefully selected target must have regular staff and quality service that values the customer. Having chosen such a venue, he should befriend the exemplary employees. He will need to become a regular customer, sitting in the same seat and ordering the same service or item each visit. He may make himself memorable by exchanging little pleasantries, but the rules explicitly prohibit dancing on the tables and bad Elvis impersonations. The goal here is to integrate, not to get arrested.

Shaken, not stirred

The cocktail: a dangerous and impossibly glamorous concoction, with an often improbable and imaginative name such as Green Vesper or Monkey Gland. These drinks, from which every right-minded liver shrinks, nonetheless conjure an image of sophisticated 1930s bars wherein Bright Young Things enriched their lives and ruined their health.

It is time that your man entered the fray and invented his own cocktail, to be launched at a sophisticated cocktail party, held at 6.00 pm and accompanied by delicious canapés and assorted nuts. (Straw hats and seersucker are optional.) He will need an exceptionally well-stocked bar, containing bourbon, whisky, cognac, gin, vodka, tequila, a small child with a lisp, Jagermeister, sake, rum, absinthe, beer, and champagne as well as coffee, chocolate, and orange liqueurs, a whole barrow of fruit, cream, crushed ice, very white teeth and a cocktail shaker.

Now did you read carefully to assert which one of those doesn't belong? Correct: Jagermeister—no one over 30 should drink the infamous German liquor. To minimize costly errors, begin by mutating an existing drink. Limit your man's trials to one cocktail a day, though. If he ignores this advice, his successful cocktail may well be named, The Fast Track to Rehab.

Tattoo you

When you were young, only sailors and the tattooed lady at the circus sported tattoos. Now you can hardly open a newspaper without seeing some celebrity display a new piece of body art.

The young have meaningful quotes etched across their bottoms, visible above the designer labels of their low-slung jeans. Roses and stars and eastern symbols are sprinkled liberally across their bodies.

So why shouldn't your guy take the plunge? But what should he choose and where should he have it? It may be too late to ink "Mother" on his forearm, and "LOVE" and "HATE" across his knuckles certainly won't please the secretary of the golf club. If your man is an ex-communist, a discreet hammer and sickle at his ankle

If he can take the pain, why not move on to piercings next? Just don't be surprized if your kids yell at you for desecrating your body.

might work. Or consider the more wearable date of retirement with a tiny carriage clock at the base of the spine, a tattoo location that is only moderately eye-clawingly agonizing to have done.

A good tattooist (with clean needles) will have a catalogue of possible designs, but perhaps your bloke could have his family crest on one pec like a blazer badge, or his last will and testament down his spine. On second thought, disregard. That might make the reading of the will fairly awkward.

Body art is as old as man and in the 21st century it's cool for everyone who wants it. If he can take the pain, why not move on to piercings next? Just don't be surprized if your kids yell at you for desecrating your body.

The old campaigner

He has paid his local and national taxes his whole life, and grumbled when he felt that they had been wrongly allocated or misspent. As a young man, he may have demonstrated (and may still, of course) against corrupt government plans and laws. These may have been "big ticket" issues, such as war, prejudice, the Big Brother state, injustice, and he and he may not have had time to lend his voice to protests closer to home, like the continued exist-ence of the show *Big Brother*.

We get the government that we deserve, and we should pay attention, or we can find ourselves living in a society we no longer recognize (but deserve). Now that he does have time, he could help to organize or support local campaigns to prevent the bulldozing of local treasures: an ancient oak tree, the Art-Deco cinema, or TV's John Cleese. He could lobby on behalf of the local museum, the library, or old person's social club, if they are under threat. He could find willing volunteers to help staff these vital services, or mastermind a letter-writing campaign to inform local and national politicians of strong objections to these measures.

Cyber-protests are an effective way of getting petitions going and obtaining signatures. Citizens who can't or won't take to the streets may be pleased to add their names online. So it's time to man the virtual barricades.

From Pacman to GTA

In his youth, your man may have flirted with Space Invaders or Pac-Man. He may have graduated to Super Mario in the 1980s, but it's been decades since he pursued such frivolous turtle-murder.

Now he has loads of time, encourage him to take on the challenge of the new "multi-player, multi-platform" world. The graphics in current games are unbelievable, like action movies but with a plot. Start with *BioShock* or *L.A. Noire* which are set in eras even older than he is. Console games play on your TV and often require an Internet connection. In *Call of Duty* (a war game) he can play alone or with others online, as members of his platoon discuss tactics and strategy in missions involving crucial skills such as finding things, destroying things, and learning new swearwords from ten-year-olds.

> **The graphics in current games are unbelievable, like action movies but with a plot.**

Movement-controlled games for Nintendo or Wii consoles offer gentler games like tennis, golf, bowling, or dance-offs—the perfect way for him to break his first hip. If it's a thrill he's after, *Grand Theft Auto* allows him to steal a variety of fast cars, shoot a lot of people, and explore his alter ego as a criminal underworld mastermind. He can also buy new clothes, eat, and go on dates, which in a weird way teaches him to enjoy the same things you do.

There but for fortune

Retired Man has raised his family and launched them into the world. He worked hard, worried, and saw them through from toys to boys (and girls), and far, far beyond. They may well be bringing up families of their own by now. Surely, he has done his bit to safeguard the future of the species? Now he has time to take a breath and look around him, he sees that all over the world, less-fortunate fathers are unable to provide food, healthcare, and education for their children. Despite their very best efforts, the odds are stacked against them. We who were lucky enough to grow up before HIV and in a Western industrialized countries, unaffected by disease, drought, and disaster have the opportunity to help those in less fortunate parts of the world to afford their children the basic rights like food, healthcare and education.

Cynics suggest we suffer from compassion fatigue, so prove them wrong with so many appeals following natural and man-made disasters, but those are one-offs mercifully. Your man can make a long-term sustained commitment to support a third-world child through school, for as little as he spent on travel to and from work in a month.

You might expect a joke here, but with utter sincerity: let's fight AIDS, ignorance, and all forms of poverty that don't produce excellent folk music and provincial cuisine.

Man Gets New Hat

There are so many ways for us to get our thoughts out into the public arena these days. We can tweet, blog, join a social network, stand on a soapbox and shout, or film ourselves standing on a soapbox shouting and put it on YouTube. But what about your local newspaper? You might think that its day has gone, but that will come as a surprise to the thousands who enjoy reading local pieces about people they know, in the traditional paper form.

Your man can research, write, and submit a news article to your local newspaper. Is there something that he feels passionate about? Perhaps, he could pen an accolade to a local personality who has contributed something extraordinary to the community? Maybe there is something shady in the latest property development scheme or something heroic in the care of the elderly (or maybe it's both, with a new housing project using the elderly as wall insulation). It's possible that one of your town's own has performed an act of great courage or compassion. Your town needs to know.

All he needs is plucky perseverance, a boy-reporter's spiral notebook, and a fedora with press card stuck in the band. If he wears a Superman costume underneath the suit, he also gets to rescue you in some bedroom roleplay, but if such shenanigans get out, that's your next front-page scandal.

Instructions?
What instructions?

When he was a little boy, your retired man was never without his penknife with its various attachments, including the legendary tool for removing stones from horse's hooves. With it, he could make the necessary adjustments to his bicycle, and screw and unscrew things when appropriate, or mischievously inappropriate. He may have had a Meccano or other construction set and he was a dab hand at pocket engineering. In those days a boy learned about the construction of the bridges and edifices of which his father was so very proud. Later, products were designed sealed modules, and then came the mystery of computerization. It's difficult for the 21st-century man to mend or make anything.

Then there are instructions—no man of any age likes to read them, unless to confirm his own decisions, believing that his total comprehension of all things mechanical is innate. If you want to give him a really pleasurable pastime, get hold of an old mechanical toaster or clockwork clock that he can repair. You can often find them in flea markets, consignment or antique shops, or yard sales.

If you want to give him a really pleasurable pastime, get hold of an old mechanical toaster or clockwork clock-doesn't-work that he can repair.

Furnish him with a screwdriver set and a small can of lubricant. Let him take the device apart, then put it back together. Be prepared for your kitchen counter to resemble the scene of a very tiny plane crash during this time. Most importantly, when he has finished, never ever hold up that odd nut or bolt to ask "Where does this piece go?"

Reality TV

In television's long history, the local stations seem to have held it a rule that their business is to report heart-warming stories of escaped (and found!) prize pigs, kittens rescued from trees, and the birthday celebrations of centenarians. Local meteorologists forecast weather and what it means for local festivities like agricultural shows and the weddings.

Now's your man's chance. Time for him to audition as a breakfast show presenter, sports reporter, or local historian, or to convince the local station to film one of the more extreme challenges he has undertaken from this very book.

Maybe he could sit in a rocking chair, wearing a wizard's hat, and read a story for children, or become a fanged Dracula.

Maybe he could sit in a rocking chair, wearing a wizard's hat, and read a story for children, or become a fanged Dracula in a leather club chair, late at night, telling ghost stories. Perhaps he could demonstrate cooking or host a gardening slot. Or maybe he could just come on and grumble or rant about local issues, as Mr Quite-Angry-Man.

Grandpa poses

He may not be the archetypical grandfather figure—no snowy white hair and little round spectacles on the end of his nose—but the chances are that Retired Man, however cool and hip he may be in designer jeans, may have grandchildren of his own by now. (If he has someone else's grandchildren, take them back to the park and schedule an appointment with the neurologist.) It is a very special relationship between grandfather and grandchild, lovely when they're babies and often bridging gaps in communication between parents and older children—a safe haven for both.

In these fast-paced times, generations sometimes get separated by geography, as young families follow the work and extended families stretch. If his grandchildren are far away, propose he hone those grandfatherly skills by becoming a surrogate grandpa to a young family nearby who are missing their own grandparents. Working parents can often do with some help at the end of the school day and they might also appreciate a night out together knowing that their children are safe with a babysitter they can rely on.

Introductions can be made by someone both families know and trust and he may offer references to reassure nervous parents. The formalities completed, he can get on with being Grandpa Joe. (Adjust accordingly if his name is Nick or Harry.)

Swan song

Now that he is no longer chained to a desk or trapped on the 7:42 train to Worksville, your retired man may want to prove useful around the home. Of course, he may have always been a domestic god, cheerfully sharing the burden of childcare, housework, cooking, and general drudgery. It is, after all, *his* universally acknowledged truth that few women can rival a man when it comes to the most efficient dishwasher stack. However, with time on his hands (which if they remain idle will certainly be put to work by the devil) he may want to lend flair and artistic creativity to even the most mundane of household tasks, like laying the table.

Whether it is to be a romantic feast for two, a glorious family celebration or a simple meal for friends, the finishing touches turn a simple meal into an occasion. Fresh flowers, crystal glasses, and silverware glinting in soft candlelight all play their part, but when it comes to dazzling your fellow diners or amusing the children, nothing can compare with a flight of swans, a dozen water lilies, or a pond of frogs, all fashioned from spotless white linen.

Encourage your man to master the art of napkin-folding. All it takes is a pile of napkins, a set of instructions downloaded from the Internet and hours and hours of quiet practice in a room at the very top of the house. Make the folder launder and iron himself, for the full experience!

Overture and beginners please

Theatre is a seductive mistress. Be warned, once Retired Man has experienced the legendary smell of the greasepaint and the roar of the crowd, he may be lost to it—enticed, or just kidnapped by a traveling troupe of troubadours. It may be too late for him to star on Broadway or London's West End, though who can say? A talent scout may take in the local production of *The Boy Friend*, and be bowled over by RM's portrayal of Mr de Thrill, or thrilled by his depiction of Mr de Bowl. Never mind, you can be his dresser.

Amateur dramatics is a popular pastime. We long to tread the boards, but we are directed into sensible, secure career choices; our dreams packed away with the dressing up clothes. Do put your chap on the stage, Ms Retired-Man; he will be amused, entertained, and charmed, and he may gain important insights about himself and the human condition.

> He could be an ugly sister, or the back end of a horse.

He could let his hair down in the traditional variety/pantomine fashion (men of a certain age have always been drawn to play the cross-dressing "dame"). He he could be an ugly sister, or the back end of a horse. Or both if this is a Beckett play. If he auditions for these parts, just remind yourself that if he looks ugly as a woman, he must make for a rugged man.

Back in the saddle

How is your chap with animals? Maybe he cherishes the family dog, and tolerates the cat (or vice versa), and perhaps he even showed some affection for the hamster before that mishap with the vacuum, but has he displayed any talent as a horse-whisperer? Is there any sign that he yearns to ride like the wind, astride a chestnut hunter with flaring nostrils and fire in his eyes.

Start by booking him some very private lessons,; he doesn't need to be humiliated by joining a class of confident and competent six-year-olds, each more confident and competent than he (that's what he has you for). He will progress from walking through to trotting, cantering and galloping, up to advanced rearing-majestically-against-the-setting-sun. When he has mastered the basics, plan an equestrian holiday, where he can put his new skills into practice in a grown up environment. Remember, it is important for him to bond with the horses, so don't excuse him from mucking out and grooming. Likewise, if he wants to bond with you, he will do his own laundry.

Now that he has conquered equestrian pursuits, he can hold his head up high in the face of those mocking six-year-olds, and compete in point to points against ten-year-olds instead.

Beer, brats
& Bavarians

Since man first settled down, beer has been important. It replaced water where the supply was impure or only patchily available. In the Middle Ages, small beer was drunk by men, women and children, with every meal and here comes a useful bit of trivia—it was largely brewed at home by women. It has long been the alcoholic choice of men, and probably yours.

Sometimes there is no substitute for a beer with the boys at a bar; other times a beer at home is perfect—so why not a beer *from* home? I know what you're thinking: messy, exploding jars of yeasty, frothy beer pouring in rivulets over the carpet. To stay on the safe side give him a designated play area, like the garage. He can brew a wide variety of flavours and strengths and share them with friends and neighbours. Why not have his own private beer festival? Talented chums can pay for their beer with musical performances, though a Bavarian Oompah band may be too much to hope for. Serve a variety of breads, cheeses, and sausage to keep the festival mood going (and soak up the alcohol), and for extra authenticity, run a hosepipe over the flower beds so mud can be tracked through the house.

A fine vintage

Over the years, and long expense account lunches, Mr RM might have developed a taste for good wine and decent whisky, (though hopefully, not for wild, wild, women.) He may now feel he will have to tighten his belt, and give up those indulgences. Such notions are undue pessimism though, as every retired man should have at least one opportunity to taste the very finest wine, champagne, or port (delete as applicable) and know the subtler pleasures of a fine, aged, single-malt whisky. Even if he wrinkles his nose and can't understand what all the fuss is about.

He should research the very best and rarest vintages of the wines he feels he might like, (or pretend to at a connoisseur's wine society.) Many such have wine-tasting evenings where, at a price, he can educate his palate and enjoy a variety of very fine wines while raising his nose in the air and proclaiming a certain vintage "resplendent in its bouquet, with notes of cardamom and a hint of superciliousness in the nose." He might attend wine auctions, just to get an idea of the value that experts place on fine wines. He might even find this out when scratching his nose accidentally procures him a $14,000 bottle. When his research is complete and his bank account emptied, he should acquire a single bottle of a rare, fine vintage to lay down for the future.

Olympic rings

Your chap is disappointed. He has been too busy to break an athletic record or qualify for an Olympic event, discipline or sport (yes, there are distinctions). Success even eludes him in Bandy and Wushu (real sports—look them up). Now the rake of lost opportunity has erased the triple jump footprints in the sandpit of time, or has it?

Although actual elite sports may be beyond him now, the world of virtual sporting achievement is still wide open.

Although actual elite sports may be beyond him now, the world of virtual sporting achievement is still wide open. Computerized, movement-activated sports and games that are played on the TV, via a games console, like those from Wii or Nintendo are not just for the young. Playing the computer is a solitary pursuit but, when hooked up them over the Internet, he could bring together his friends, and even strangers, to compete in golf, tennis, bowls, boxing, soccer, baseball and others in an "armchair Olympics."

Elimination rounds could culminate in a grand final. Perhaps he has some spare gold, silver, and bronze behind the couch cushions that he can have struck into medals. Box these up and mail them to the victors while humming the gold medalist's national anthem, all without ever leaving the living room.

Hometown tourist

It is a curious phenomenon that we can live and work in a town or city for a lifetime, yet never see its streets and churches, museums or markets as they might look to a stranger. It is very easy to become blinded as we go about the daily grind, noses to the grindstone, shoulders to the wheel, and other clichés.

Now that he has retired, your fellow might like to rediscover his own small part of the universe, in all its glory. The first step is to book a nice B&B close to home for the weekend, as if he were indeed a tourist. Let him try the complementary tea and coffee-making facilities and perhaps a trouser press before enjoying a breakfast prepared by someone else (other than you). Now it's time to start his tour!

Armed with a street map marked with interesting places, and perhaps some tourism leaflets, he sets out to revisit the local history. If his phone does not have a camera, a disposable will do. Diversify his weekend! There are always museums and galleries to explore, food or flea markets to sample, and a cozy chapel or marvellous cathedral. If he looks up occasionally, he may discover architectural gems not yet obliterated by the neon shop fronts at eye level.

When he comes home he can show you his snaps and recount his adventures while you dispose of his touristy baseball cap discreetly.

Tiny topiary

Who among us has not been amazed, or at least amused by "the horticultural practice of training live perennial plants, by clipping the foliage and twigs to develop clearly defined shapes, perhaps geometric or fanciful;" the art of topiary?

Perhaps he doesn't have room for an elaborate living sculpture on his balcony, but your green-fingered man could while away his newfound leisure nurturing a tiny maze of watercress in a seed tray. If he has a sense of humour, fashion him a wire model of a chicken, pot it, and watch him tend a climbing ivy or jasmine as it grows through the wire, which he may snip it into shape. In time, rabbits, ducks, snails, an elephant, a giraffe, or an entire menagerie tended by tiny people, grown from box, could join the chicken.

Is it art or is it gardening? That answer must come from within the caretaker's soul. Still, it is the perfect pastime for a control freak, bending even Mother Nature to his will, in his own, small way.

Will you welcome, please...

It cannot have escaped your notice that stand-up comedy is the new rock and roll. Your man deserves his share of the fame and glory. Who is it that has the children rolling in the aisles (why does your home have aisles?) and your parents wiping tears from their tired old eyes? He is the life and soul of every party and the hero of the locker room. Now he has the time and the opportunity to perfect his act, seek out new material, and even take his show on the road. Every pub has an open mic night these days and this is his opportunity to showcase his talent before a very discerning audience. Is he brave enough to face hecklers and the potential rejection?

Persuade him not to start any joke with "I say, I say, I say," or "Have you ever noticed...?" nor to embark on a shaggy dog story that burns his allotted time. The observational one-liner always does well, and even the worst cracker pun gets a laughing groan. Finally, however much he begs, do not agree to be his straight man.

Eco-skilled

He may be a wiz with the cordless screwdriver, an ace painter and decorator, and a dab hand with the garden shears. But could your guy construct a hurdle fence without nails or screws, or build a garden shed with straw bales? Could he make a playhouse for his grandchildren out of willow, or manufacture his own wattle and daub plaster, or lime wash paint?

Now is a good time to learn skills which depend on human energy rather than fossil fuelpower.

Well, probably not. Why should he be able to do these things, they are arcane and age-old and there are probably only a few hundred craftsmen who can teach others to master them in the Western hemisphere? Precisely those reasons is why. Now is a good time to learn skills which depend on human energy rather than fossil fuelpower.

Persuade your man to take a course or two. The learning process will be fun and he will graduate with impeccable eco cred to his children and grandchildren. Make sure that he wears protective clothing if he works with lime, and you should be careful to resist his blandishments when it comes to taking up residence in the straw bale shed and handing the house over to the children.

Checkmate!

Does your man imagine himself growing into one of those venerable old guys sitting in the Town Square or local coffee shop, playing his weekly game of chess with his boyhood friend, as they have done these past 50 years? In this dream he looks much more wizened and Mediterranean and smokes Turkish cigarettes or Gauloise. It is now time for you to call his bluff, by insisting—yes, insisting—that he actually live this dream, at least in part, by first learning to play chess, and then tracking down a boyhood friend with whom he can play each week.

Chess is a fabulous game of consummate skill, intelligence, and strategy, which can be played by people of all ages, and Retired Man will love it. There are set-piece, classic games to study, books to read, and strategies to memorize. Endless chess sets are available for any man's taste, from the land of Mordor and the terracotta army to beautiful traditional pieces with inlaid boards. In the summer, you could give him a giant, outdoor set to play with, combining intellectual and physical exercise, and he could start his own all-season chess club. On those rainy days, leaving the house is no impediment. Mr Internet-Savvy can play virtual chess in that café/bar, with venerable foreign gentlemen, each more wizened than the last, as he sips his own, quite real, cognac and perfects his accent.

Inner peace and snake hips

As we get older our bodies become disobedient. Hearts and lungs, which worked perfectly for years, suddenly start to slow up a little and joints become less supple. Years of sedentary office work do not help. You want to keep your retiree in peak fitness, however much he would like to put his feet up and take an afternoon nap.

Heavy gym regimes are not ideal for older bodies, but there is no reason why he shouldn't keep up his strength and stamina and achieve that inner peace which always eluded him on the commute to the office. Yoga is the perfect answer. It stretches the muscles, works towards balance, and keeps joints supple. The repetition and pace, often coupled with gentle meditation, soothes and calms the mind. That's Day 1.

On Day 2, sign him up for something a little more strenuous and aerobic to give the heart and lungs a decent workout. Zumba is the answer! Zumba is a Latin dance fitness programme created by Colombian choreographer Alberto "Beto" Perez in the 1990s. It is fast, infectious, with really great music and more like a party than a workout. You should go too, as there is every possibility that he will come home with the spirit of a Latin lover and the energy to match. Keep up at the back there!

Doggy day care

Now that he has retired, are you finding it difficult to get your man out of the house for a breath of fresh air and a little light exercise? Would he love a dog to take him for walks?

When you were both away from home all day, you probably didn't feel that it would be either kind or responsible to keep a dog alone in the house from morning till night. Even though you are both around now, he is reluctant to make the commitment. You are just beginning this phase of your lives and you want to be free to travel, but he would still love a dog to take for walks and for whom to throw a ball or Frisbee in the park.

Doggy day care is the solution you seek. Sign your retired man up for training as a dog-handler (not the attack dog kind!) to competently control multiple dogs in a public place. Take a trip to your local pet supplies store and invest in a pooper-scoop and an economy size pack of disposal bags. Buy a selection of durable balls and other toys, and a selection of healthy dog treats. Now, he is all set to advertise as a dogsitter for pet owners who have to leave their dogs alone. No more excuses, job done.

If his newfound skills lead you as a couple to adopt a dog of your own, please do consider saving a rescue dog from a shelter.

Guerilla gardening

Last year, over 6,000 people signed up for International Guerilla-gardening Sunflower Day, and planted seed in abandoned areas of earth, in towns and cities all over the Northern hemisphere. In due season, surprised and delighted citizens awoke to find these optimistic blooms piercing the gloom of their urban environment. Could your retiree be tempted to put a lifetime's gardening expertise to good use by joining others to "seed bomb" and "pavement pimp" his own locale as a guerilla gardener?

In this day and age, urban space for vegetables, herbs, and flowers is at a premium, with waiting lists for allotments growing like the weeds they have torn out. Neglected land fills the corners of every town and city, from the unplanted pits around trees and shrubs in tubs in shopping malls to abandoned housing estates awaiting redevelopment. These are put to temporary or permanent good use by those with horticultural skills and time to share them. Groups organize themselves with poster campaigns or Internet networking sites to gather gardeners, tools, and seeds to cultivate these plots. At midnight—they strike! A word of caution: guerilla gardeners can be accused of trespass, so if at all possible, the permission of the landowner should be gained. It is difficult to see how anyone can object to the generosity of green-thumbed eco-activists, who grow food and share the harvest while improving the environment.

Duct tape art

If your chap has ever fixed anything around the house, he is likely the proud possessor of duct tape. Curiously, if he's fixed ducts, the use of the self-same-named tape is against building regulations. Known in the arts as "gaffer," this strong, flexible, tacky (in the sticky sense) tape comes in a variety of widths and a rainbow of colours and has a myriad of very sensible uses. NASA astronauts are even reputed to have used it for emergency repairs aboard Apollo 13! However, we need not concern ourselves with its practical applications, since we are interested only in its creative potential as a material with which to work artistically, and thus fill the days of our man's retirement with joyous endeavour.

Fashionistas will confirm that a duct-tape top hat is the very height of millinery chic.

Google "duct tape art and crafts" and you will be staggered at the results, from a "duct-tape turtle" to a "duct tape mini-skirt." Duck Products, the manufacturer of Duck brand duct tape, annually sponsors a competition that offers a college scholarship to the person who creates the most stylish formalwear made from Duck Tape. At last, a way to help out a grandchild with college fees! Of course he can create pictures, models, and sculpture too, and fashionistas will confirm that a duct-tape top hat is the very height of millinery chic. As well they should, after it paid their tuition to design school.

Flashmob

The first few months of retirement can seem a little strange, accustomed as your retiree is to being part of a crowd. After a while, the unalloyed joy of being in one another's pockets might begin to pall, sadly, and he may yearn to be part of a crowd again. Solution: he should start a flashmob.

They could sing, dance, pillow fight or do acrobatics or silent disco.

A flashmob is a group of people who, organized through social networking sites, assemble suddenly in a public space, perform an unusual or apparently pointless act and then disperse. The first gathered in Manhattan in 2003, as a social experiment. Flashmobs have since become major international events.

All your chap needs is a cellphone or Facebook page to gather a group, decide on a theme and a location, and organize rehearsals. They could sing, dance, pillow fight or do acrobatics or silent disco. Everyone must be perfectly synchronized. At the appointed time, the mob mingles with a crowd, as if strangers to one another. On signal, everyone begins the performance, then at the end; simply go on their way. Flashmobs—the perfect way to be alone in a crowd.

Geocaching

Are you overjoyed at the advent of satellite navigation? Have you said goodbye to map-reading misery and tense journeys, where he loses his temper if you get lost and he won't ask for directions? Isn't it strange the way men love maps? If yours also has a passion for mysterious quests, codes, and co-ordinates; if he is a geek or a gadget freak, then he will love geocaching.

A geocacher places a waterproof container containing a log book (with pen or pencil) and items for trade at a specific location anywhere in the world, then records the cache's coordinates. These co-ordinates, along with other details of the location, are posted on a listing site where other geocachers pick them up and seek out the cache using their GPS handheld receivers. The finding geocachers record their exploits in the log book and online.

Geocachers are free to take objects (except the logbook, pencil, or stamp) from the cache in exchange for leaving something of similar or higher value. Typical cache "treasures" are not high in monetary value but may hold personal value to the finder. Aside from the log book, common cache contents are unusual coins or currency, small toys, ornamental buttons, CDs, or books. Other

common objects
that are moved from
cache to cache are called
"hitchhikers" such as Travel
Bugs or Geocoins, whose travels may be logged and followed online.

For like-minded souls, this hi-tech treasure hunting is the perfect
long distance and hands-on hobby. You may need to place a trace on
him too, just to keep track.

Massage in a bottle

However fit and toned your retiree might be, there will be times when your full and busy retirement leaves you both longing for a good, long soak in a nice, hot tub. Some of the more strenuous challenges in this book could leave you with the occasional aching muscle too and, even in retirement, there are worries and stresses that cause tight muscles and tension headaches.

This challenge is for your retiree to make his own aromatherapy massage oil and the two of you learn to give one another safe but effective massages. This is not the hippie version that purports to cure trauma of the chakras. This is a manly pursuit, much like having a chemistry set in his childhood: nice little dark bottles, a mixing beaker, pipettes, and a resulting mixture which smells significantly better than sulfur. With 100ml of sweet almond oil as the base oil, add two drops each of lavender, rosemary, frankincense and chamomile. Gently shake.

If either of you is allergic to scents, just use warmed baby or massage oil, and for pete's sake, stay upwind of bakeries. It is advisable to get proper instruction in the art of massage for both safety and capability, so sign both of you up for a good course in the therapeutic method of your choice: Swedish, Shiatsu, Hot Stone, Thai, Reflexology, Head, and Back massage are all popular forms at the moment.

Marathon man

First, there was school cross-country running: cold days, wet feet and that smug so-and-so McFitster always winning. (We know you're reading this, McFitster!) Then came jogging, a tracksuit-clad, bandana-wearing 1980s sport. Now, there is distance running, and despite past trauma, your man will love it. He can't start without a clean bill of health and then he *must* train slowly to build his fitness and stamina. Remind him that his task here is not to run to the limit of his abilities, but rather to survey them.

Fast forward: he is a lean, fit, running machine, but now he needs pals to run alongside—stalking horses if you will, or someone slower to fall behind when the wolves come at them. He should join a club. He will enjoy the friendly banter so familiar from the office water cooler. This is his gateway to entering local fun-runs. Many are sponsored for charity and are truly worthwhile.

His chief problem will be the motivation to train. Set the alarm for bright and early (just like the work days) and line up his running shoes where his slippers used to rest. Wash his shorts and vest (remember: no starch). Get him some manly shower gel called something like "jaguar" or "wolf" and some power bars for breakfast. Wave him off with a proud smile and a bottle of water. Oh, and never let him dress as a chicken or any kind of vegetable.

Run away and join the circus

Well, not actually run away, but for the little boy trapped inside most men this has always remained a dream. But your chap has probably come to love his creature comforts, and touring the country in a caravan might have lost its allure. He can still boast great hand-eye coordination though, and while some of the most dangerous circus skills are beyond him now, (trapeze and lion taming are best learned in childhood), he could still study some big top arts.

A few lucky locales have a circus school where he can meet some interesting people, master the unicycle, and pass as a bearded lady. A skill like stilt-walking will make him feel ten feet tall (literally) and has domestic applications like reaching the back of the high kitchen cupboards without difficulty, so that's a bonus.

He may need some tights (yes, I know), spangly leo-tards, huge shoes, and baggy trousers, but you can some room in the wardrobe by donating his old suits to charity. The juggling balls, spinning plates, and clown car can all go in the garage when not in use. As ever, you may need to provide a soft landing place for him to practise, but you're used to that by now.